MW00620898

The Liberty Solution

In Liberty,

Derek Wills

Derek R. Wills

Foreword by Walter Block, Ph.D

Copyright © 2021 Derek R. Wills

All rights reserved. No part of this publication may be reproduced in any manner whatsoever without the written permission of the publisher except in the case of reprints in the context of reviews.

Published by Gentlemen For Liberty

For information, email Gentlemen For Liberty at Gents4Liberty@protonmail.com

Paperback ISBN: 978-1-7373783-0-3
Ebook ISBN: 978-1-7373783-1-0

Dedicated to my beautiful wife, Dacia.

Thank you for all of your love and support.

Table of Contents

Foreword

This is a welcome book in the literature of liberty. It is written from the heart and soul. You will not find reams of statistics in this book. The author is not (yet!!!) a famous scholar. He has no Ph.D.

What you will find is inspiration. You will be enervated to get "out there" and spread the word.

Derek Wills starts out at the very beginning by asking "What is liberty," and by offering an important answer. This alone is worth the entire price of admission. He then follows up with an important discussion of one of the bedrocks of liberty, private property rights, and how the all-loving state has been seriously denigrating them. Only a serious libertarian could entitle one of his chapters: "Taxation is Not Theft... It is Extortion." I am not sure that I fully agree with him on this matter, but I am delighted to report that I never thought of the matter in this way before, and have learned, mightily, from his discussion of these concepts.

He makes a crucially important distinction between crony capitalism and laissez faire capitalism. It is necessary to do this since all too many people confuse the two concepts. They think that what we have now is "capitalism" and quite correctly want no part of this system created and enjoyed by the denizens of the Washington DC "swamp" along with the capital cities of all 50 states, to say nothing of the mayors, city council members, etc., who are busily destroying our freedoms.

Our author spares no ammunition in taking to task one of his mentor's (Ron Paul) least favorite institution, the Fed. Seemingly innocuous to most people, this institution drops no bombs on anyone, shoots no rockets, and fires no bullets at innocent people. But it enables these evil activities, and to add insult to injury, creates the business cycle, unemployment, and inflation. Mr. Wills is quite right in targeting central banking.

I was very taken with his treatment of the right to life. At the outset, I thought he would be discussing the abortion issue. He does, but he does so much more. Consider this one sentence: "Bob is sitting at a bus stop when Jack decides to shoot and kill him. Is life a natural right?" You know what this reminds me of? Call me a weirdo, but it brings to mind the simplicity (Occam's Razor appreciates this sort of thing) with which Hazlitt, in his world-famous "Economics in One Lesson" deals with the complexity of the dismal science. Slowly building up to a crescendo, Wills brings into the discussion the unjustified murders of the Nazis and the very different death penalty for vicious killers of innocents.

There is no incompatibility between libertarian theory and the incarceration of real criminals. In his chapter on the injustice system, Wills bewails the incarceration of victimless criminals, those found guilty of what Robert Nozick has characterized as "capitalist acts between consenting adults." He notes that the U.S. is the world's leader in imprisonment rates, to our shame.

This book is rounded out by incisive discussions of immigration, international relations (bring those troops home!), money and environmentalism.

Mr. Wills and I disagree on animal rights. However, his discussion of this topic, a pattern found all throughout this book, is nothing less than electrifying.

I recommend that all libertarians purchase not one, but several copies of this book, the first to read and then reread, the others to pass along to friends, family members and acquaintances. If liberty is to be bequeathed to our children and grandchildren, it will be done by books of this sort: beautifully written, erudite, informational. If there are any important issues not covered in this short volume, I'd have a hard time thinking of what they might be. He really covers the waterfront of liberty.

Dr. Walter Block

Preface

L iberty. She is an ideal taken for granted each and every day in the United States. She is recited in the National Anthem and Pledge of Allegiance, and she is the single most important tenet on which the Founding Fathers gave birth to the United States of America. Americans have grown numb over the years to her well-being because it seems to be accepted without any doubt whatsoever that she will always be the very foundation of American culture. Unfortunately, American liberty is but a shadow of her former self. As a millennial, I am deeply troubled by the fact that I have never known liberty, and through my love of history, I can say affirmatively that my grandparents' generation didn't truly know her either.

I have always been passionate about history, and the more I learned, the more I realized just how many of our freedoms have been taken from us. I do not say this as a Republican or a Democrat. In fact, I am neither of those things. I am a libertarian in the truest sense and am not loyal to any political party, including the Libertarian Party. Please, do not allow that admission to let any prejudice cloud the intentions of this treatise. While chances are high that those reading these pages are already liberty-minded, what has been written here is a message for everyone, and it is my genuine hope that those who are now indoctrinated into statism will read this with an open mind. It does not matter if you are a progressive Democrat, a constitutional conservative, a socialist, a Republican, a libertarian, or anything else around the political compass; the message of liberty is meant for you, as it is your natural right, and this message is meant to be spread.

That is not to suggest that you will agree with everything contained in these pages. Quite the contrary. While all Americans express their genuine love for liberty, nearly everyone admits to supporting laws and regulations that infringe on liberties of other individuals in one form or other. That doesn't make them bad people or un-American. When tyranny and statism are all a people have ever known, it becomes nearly impossible to understand the true concept of liberty. It has, in many instances, actually been conveyed as a scary notion; that a state of liberty will mean certain death for some and unlimited power for others. It is quite depressing when one realizes that the greatest gift from God (or nature, depending on your beliefs) is something that all too many people fear, thanks to propagandists.

I am no one special. I am merely a concerned individual who cares deeply about liberty for all, including the liberty with which I disagree. I see the tyrannies committed by agents of the state, as they oppress people they claim to protect and serve. What's more, I see many people supporting this oppression based on their religious or philosophical beliefs, which I find to be deplorable. After living through and serving in the military under the tyranny of the Obama Administration, I watched dumbfounded as Republicans across the country approved the nomination of Donald Trump, a man who had written about his support for gun control, and who had donated large sums of money to Democratic candidates running for various offices. Shortly thereafter, I began my advocacy for liberty by signing on as a writer for Lone Star Gun Rights. In 2017, I began hosting LSGR's weekly podcast, and though my advocacy was then limited to gun rights, the issue of liberty was my main motivation. I ultimately resigned from LSGR in 2020, and helped launch a new podcast called Gentlemen, For Liberty.

I was inspired to write this after a speech I gave at a gun rights rally in Santa Fe, TX following the tragic shooting at Santa Fe High School. I was incredibly humbled by the compliments I received on my speech, one of which was, "You need to write a book." I made it my mission the following day to write a book in hopes of conveying a message of liberty to everyone wishing to read it. Throughout my journey in writing this treatise, I discovered just how rampant tyranny is in the United States. With all of the issues at the forefront of political commentary in our country, I often find myself asking why liberty is never presented as an option. Every problem seems to be caused by the state's involvement in our lives, so it's not farfetched to believe that liberty is not only a solution to each problem, but the main or only solution.

This treatise is what many will call (and have called) "extreme." In the most literal of definitions, they would technically be correct; however, I reject the notion that the ideas of self-ownership and natural rights are fallacious. What are portrayed in this treatise are not new ideas. Everything is built upon the ideas of liberty-minded philosophers, scholars, and intellectuals who came before me, and since liberty itself is a gift from nature, everything written on these pages is as old as mankind itself.

In order for liberty and her message to thrive, it is imperative that we as individuals reject any and all notions of philosophical hypocrisy, even if that means we must adopt a view that we do not personally like in one area in order to keep consistency across the entire spectrum. This is one of the biggest issues across the world, and it is the root cause of most, if not all, of the tyrannies that run rampant. I will not lie and tell you that it will be easy. For some, it might be. For others, it will not. When I began this project, there were many positions I was forced to change by the time it was completed in order to do that very thing. Intellectual honesty is absolutely necessary if liberty is going to be saved from her deathbed.

Part I:
Grievances Against the State

Chapter 1

What is Liberty?

"I prefer dangerous liberty to peaceful servitude." – Thomas Jefferson

I t seems silly to anyone to pose a question with such a ridiculous sentiment, but I challenge you to ask your peers to define liberty. Chances
are, most will begin by citing the Bill of Rights in their own words, or
saying it means we live in a free country. Some may even lead off by saying
something along the lines of, "To me, liberty is…" Herein lies one of the
single biggest problems that is legitimately plaguing the American culture.

When an individual defines liberty as they see fit, their definition
will invariably be incompatible with another individual. For example,
someone who is pro-choice will say that it is liberty for the government
to recognize the woman's right to choose to terminate her pregnancy,
whereas someone who is pro-life will say that it is liberty for the state to
recognize the unborn child's right to live, and thus restrict (if not outright prevent) the pregnant woman from getting an abortion. Liberty
will never thrive if what she looks like is not the same for every individual. Liberty is not fluid, and she does not change her looks with the times,
or from person to person. Liberty is natural, and concrete. Her definition
must be one that is universal to every individual on the planet, and so she
must be defined as follows:

> *"The right of the individual to invoke sole dominion over their own life
> to act as they see fit, provided the act in and of itself does not directly
> infringe on the right of another individual to do the same."*

This is what liberty looks like in panorama, and she is beautiful.
Or is she? The proper description of her insinuates that others will act in
a manner with which you will personally disagree; sometimes, even to a

deplorable, and morally abhorrent level. True liberty is not beautiful in all of her features. Liberty is not a privilege to be granted on the basis that one makes good decisions, nor is liberty subject to popularity. Liberty is not the Veteran's Day parade down Main St. with American Flags and red, white, and blue confetti while Lee Greenwood's "God Bless the USA" plays over the loudspeaker. True liberty is burning the American flag in protest at that parade. While most Americans, particularly conservatives, would find it disgusting to disrespect the flag of the United States in such a destructive manner, we as individuals must maintain intellectual honesty if we are going to believe in liberty to our core. To wish such acts to be punishable by the state is tyrannical. Tyranny is still tyranny even if we personally agree with its premise. No matter what excuse one makes, bringing someone to think, act, or speak the way you do by coercion is not what liberty is about.

This is precisely why we should always err on the side of liberty in all things, especially when the liberty we do not like is attacked. After all, the liberty that needs the most protection is the liberty that is the least popular. If we are content with any level of government infringing on individual liberties with which we disagree, then it would be illogical for us to be upset for them infringing on those liberties with which we do agree. All one must do is turn on any of the mainstream news channels to see story after story of individual liberty being trampled on by a state entity. It does not matter if the state is attempting to coerce a baker into baking a cake for a wedding between two consenting men who love each other, or if a state court upholds a ban on AR-15 platforms, if liberty and natural law were the standard we as a culture applied to everyday dealings, these problems would not exist.

There is a difference, however, between natural rights (those that exist in the pure absence of the state) and state-given "rights." The three fundamental natural rights with which everyone is familiar are life, liberty, and property; however, the state tends to grant "rights" as a benefit of holding the status of citizen. Since the state is the grantor of these "rights," however, they are subject to whatever stipulations the state may wish to instill upon them. When one really thinks about it, these are not really rights at all, but are instead privileges.

Voting, for example, is state-given and is not a right that is inherent to us as human beings. It is entirely dependent on the form of government instituted within the borders of a nation. Vatican City, for example, is a theocratic sovereign nation where the Pope is elected by the Conclave of cardinal electors. None of the 1,000 citizens living in Vatican City have the "right" to vote as the state has not granted such a "right" to its citizens.

There is a notion commonly accepted by American thought (though not actually put into practice) that when the state exists, the authority of the state is or should be derived entirely from the consent of the governed. After all, to place the state in a station superior to that of the individual is the first step the former takes to implement tyranny. In theory, as long as this truth is realized, and the level between the state and the individual maintains equilibrium, the form of government instituted in a nation ultimately does not matter. In practice, however, power corrupts, and a state with anything less than a perfect system of checks and balances invariably becomes lustful for more power.

Because natural rights exist in the absence of the state, these rights are each individual's birthright, and are not subject to regulation, infringement, or prohibition. What has become prevalent in American politics, however, is that the line between natural rights and morality becomes blurred. Liberty (the act of exercising one's natural rights) and morality (that which is deemed "good" and "bad" by an individual) are not the same thing, though they can (and do) coexist in a society. Both have the unique attribute that neither can be legislated into existence. A state body cannot write a new law to conjure liberty for the people. Only the full repeal of an existing law can have that effect. Similarly, the state also cannot write a law that will invoke a moral compass onto every person. While liberty is absolute, morality is relative to the individual. This sentiment is invariably met with the challenge that homicide is illegal because it is immoral, and this is the crux of why the line between the two gets blurred.

While certainly all of us would agree that killing someone in cold blood is an immoral act, homicide is illegal because that act directly infringes on the victim's natural right to live. As such, the crime of murder is an act that is considered criminal under both man's law and the laws of nature. An act can be both immoral *and* infringe on another person's liberty simultaneously. In fact, every act that violates the laws of nature, that is every act infringes on individual liberty, is immoral; however, some acts that are considered immoral by most people do not harm anyone. As an example, take the act of drinking alcohol to excess on a daily basis. Many people believe this to be an immoral act; however, since it does not in and of itself violate another person's liberty, it must be concluded that it is, in fact, a natural right.

People try and oppose this view by suggesting that the intoxicated person could act recklessly, and in doing so, harm someone else. In such a case, the assaultive or negligent action the person took to cause injury to another would be just as illegal regardless of their level of sobriety. Criminalizing the previous act of being intoxicated does nothing but violate the liberty of everyone else who wished to do so while harming no one. Because of this, it must be considered tyrannical to prohibit any individual from exercising their natural right to be a drunkard. Some may suggest that being a drunkard is at minimum harmful to the drinker, and because of this reason, regulating how much someone may drink in a given timespan is a means of preserving his right to life. The problem, however, is that only an individual owns himself. Our lives and our bodies are our own property. If any other individual, or group of individuals, has the authority over what you may or may not put into your own body, then the bearer of that authority has proclaimed itself master over you. It is this logic that strikes down any notion of validity concerning laws designed to protect an individual from himself. If the state is given the authority to prohibit any individual, or even the entire population at-large, from drinking alcohol, then every person subject to that prohibition becomes a slave to the state. Slavery is by its very definition the antithesis of liberty, and thus slavery and tyranny are entirely interchangeable.

Regardless of if you are religious or secular, the same rule still applies. By virtue of simply being human, we are endowed with the natural right of free will. This invariably includes the right to act conversely to religious teachings, even as a religious person. The state should not be instituted to uphold the moral compass of religion and invoke its wrath on those who fail to comply. Unlike liberty, tyranny comes in varying degrees of severity. While it is most often associated with overwhelming

oppression from the state, small infringements that cause mild incon-
veniences (e.g. bureaucracies) are also forms of tyranny. To illustrate the
relationship between liberty and tyranny, think of liberty as the natural
spring that quenches the thirst of our lives. In her pure and natural state,
she is unpolluted by any contaminants that could range in consequences
from giving the water a bitter taste, to making it deadly to consume.
In today's America, the spring of liberty has been polluted by so much
corruption, bureaucracy, crony capitalism, and other toxins that, should
people like Thomas Jefferson attempt to drink, he would surely be instantly repulsed by the abhorrent taste and noxious stench that met him.
He would be so disgusted by merely being within proximity of the smell,
that the water would never touch his lips. The current living generations,
on the other hand, having grown up accustomed to these toxic impurities, are entirely blind to the truth of what she is supposed to be, for we
know not what pure spring water is like. Remaining ignorant of these
impurities, whether intentional or not, is the very reason tyranny ever
comes to exist in the first place, and it is this ignorance that dooms what
freedoms Americans have lost thus far to be lost forever.

As liberty is such a precious gift from nature, it should not only
be protected, but restored to the way nature intended. Throughout global
history, states have a perfect track record of being tyrannical. The sad truth
is that today's United States government is way too powerful of an entity,
having robbed us of our natural rights under the premise of security, charity, fear, and hate. It is up to us as individuals to restore liberty, as she will
not come back on her own. The state will not willingly give us back the
natural right to act according to our own will and desire, but we do have
the power to take it back. We must break the shackles of servitude to the
various monopolies of the state and ensure we maintain intellectual honesty about our positions. This means we must acknowledge the existence
of, and fight for the restoration of, even those liberties with which we do
not agree. If we all as individuals unite behind the ideas of liberty and natural law, and force ourselves to let go of any fear we may have, we can not
only restore liberty, but also revive her to the way nature intended.

It is up to us as individuals to make the decisions necessary. If each
of us waits to act until we see others begin taking the first steps, then we

are doomed to the status quo. This means we must divest ourselves of the labels of political factions and heed President Washington's warning that they will, and have, "become potent engines, by which cunning, ambitious, and unprincipled men will be enabled to subvert the power of the people and to usurp for themselves the reins of government."[1] We can no longer sit idly by, and make excuses for our elected officials while they continue to support past usurpations and and enact new, more egregious usurpations. It is well-past time that we begin to understand what liberty truly is, and make her our top priority, regardless of what political faction to which we belong. The power we as individuals have is truly amazing; we just need to utilize it. Liberty will only die if we let her. We need to stand united as a group of individuals with a common goal in order to ensure liberty's survival. We must commit to her well-being entirely. Let us reignite her torch and fight for that very tenet upon which the United States was founded. As Jefferson Smith said in the 1939 film *Mr. Smith Goes to Washington*, "Liberty is too precious a thing to be buried in books... Men should hold it up in front of them every single day of their lives and say: I'm free..."

---

1   Washington, George (1796). "Farewell Address." Retrieved from avalon.law.yale.edu/18th_century/washing.asp

Chapter 2

Destruction of Property

---

*"Whenever legislators endeavor to take away and destroy
the property of the people, or to reduce them to slavery
under arbitrary power, they put themselves in a state
of war with the people, who are thereupon absolved
from any further obedience."*
– John Locke

John Locke should be one of the most celebrated philosophers in the United States. His ideas regarding our natural rights to life, liberty, and property were so revolutionary and inspiring, that they are rooted deeply in America's founding documents, including the Declaration of Independence. There is a misunderstanding of history believed by many that in the original draft, the Committee of Five (which consisted of Thomas Jefferson, Benjamin Franklin, John Adams, Roger Sherman, and Robert Livingston) had written "life, liberty, and property," only to change it later to "life, liberty, and the pursuit of happiness." In actuality, not only did it originally say "the pursuit of happiness," but Locke inspired this phrase as well.

In his 1689 work, An Essay Concerning Human Understanding, Locke wrote the following:

> *"The necessity of pursuing true happiness [is] the foundation of liberty. As therefore the highest perfection of intellectual nature lies in a careful and constant pursuit of true and solid happiness; so the care of ourselves, that we mistake not imaginary for real happiness, is the necessary foundation of our liberty. The stronger ties we have to an unalterable pursuit of happiness in general, which is our greatest good, and which, as such, our desires always follow, the more are we*

free from any necessary determination of our will to any particular action..." [2]

Locke's philosophy was that true liberty was intertwined with life and property, the latter of which was the product of our labor conducted in our pursuits of happiness. To Locke, property ownership, both land and goods, were as fundamental and natural to each and every person on earth as our individual lives were. The state did not bestow upon us our right to live, and no one would argue such a ridiculous notion, yet we constantly see attacks on property ownership in various forms today. Sadly, most of these are written off by those who are not affected by the infringement. It is as if there is a commonly accepted belief that one's right to property is not endowed upon one from the same pre-political source as our right to life, unless the individual experiencing such tyranny is either oneself or a loved one.

These justifications partly stem from the extensive study of, and the misguided beliefs in another philosophy: that of Karl Marx. The rise of the "democratic socialist" movement is, and of right ought to be, one of major concern for any liberty-loving individual, especially when one considers that Senator Bernie Sanders would have actually won the 2016 Democratic Presidential Primary if not for the Democratic National Committee rigging the election process in favor of former Secretary of State Hillary Clinton. [3] Socialism, whether so-called "democratic" or authoritarian, is rooted on the redistribution of wealth in order to function, but that is not the ultimate goal. By its very nature and definition, socialism goes against all of Locke's philosophy by taking the fruit of one's labor (private property) and giving it to the community as a whole. This redistribution, when done by the state through force, is called communism, and this authoritarian form of socialism is the only way to get the philosophy to "work" in a population of more than a dozen or so people. The real goal of socialism is perfectly explained by Marx himself in his 1848 work, The Communist Manifesto:

---

2   Locke, John (1689). *"An Essay Concerning Human Understanding."* Book II. Chapter XXII.
3   Martin, Jonathan; Rappeport, Alan (July 24, 2016). „Debbie Wasserman Schultz to Resign D.N.C. Post". *The New York Times.*

"The distinguishing feature of Communism is not the abolition of property generally, but the abolition of bourgeois property. But modern bourgeois private property is the final and most complete expression of the system of producing and appropriating products, that is based on class antagonisms, on the exploitation of the many by the few. In this sense, the theory of the Communists may be summed up in the single sentence: Abolition of private property." [4]

If private property is abolished, or even just the private ownership of property by the middle class, or "bourgeois" as Marx called them, liberty can never truly exist. Property is the foundation of all natural rights, as it is the one thing that gives ultimate sovereignty to an individual. When property is rightfully owned, it is utilized at the property owner's discretion, and no one else's. Regardless of whether the property is money, goods, land, or even one's own self, the right to dictate it comes solely from the property owner.

The right to property ownership cannot be anything less than a natural right. After all, under communism, by abolishing private property ownership, there can be no such thing as theft, trespassing, or even extortion since all property invariably belongs to the community at-large (i.e. the state). Personal wealth becomes extinct, and the fruits of one's labor is enjoyed by everyone equally. This invariably strips away the driving force behind self-motivation, and propels the entire population into a state of sloth. After all, why would anyone want to work hard if they will reap the same rewards as one who does nothing? This can actually be seen in one of the renowned cities of the United States: San Francisco, CA.

San Francisco's homeless problem has been a major political issue for decades, dating back to the mid 1970s. [5] Today, the problem has grown to such a high level (almost 1% of the total population), that the amount of human feces and used hypodermic needles in the streets warranted national news coverage. [6] As the homeless population continues

---

4   Marx, Karl; Engles, Friedrich (February 1848). *The Communist Manifesto*. Chapter II.

5   Green, Matthew. (June 26, 2017). "TIMELINE: The Frustrating Political History of Homelessness in San Francisco". *KQED News*.

6   Meads, Timothy. (July 14, 2028). "Major Bummer: San Francisco is Absolutely

to surge in the San Francisco Bay Area, the city has tried combating the problem by redistributing upwards of $275 million in taxpayer property.[7] In fact, programs have been so lucrative for the homeless that per the San Francisco Human Services Agency's website, homeless people in the Bay Area can receive the following benefits:

- Cash assistance of up to $606 per month
- Access to job preparation, assessments, training, and employment counseling, including:
  - Sign-up for the Voluntary Intensive Employment Services (VIES) program.
  - Immediate access to the JobsNOW! program.
  - Placement in a job with a guaranteed starting pay of at least $14 per hour.
- Education support and classes for GED, ESL, and High School Diploma.
- Opportunities for housing or shelter placement, if needed.
- Free monthly MUNI fast pass (public transportation).
- One-time assistance obtaining a free California DMV Identification Card.
- Assistance applying for free medical insurance (Medi-Cal) and food assistance (CalFresh – $194 per month).
- Assistance applying for Supplemental Security Income (SSI) from on-site case managers, if you have a long-term disability.
- Counseling for mental health, substance abuse, and domestic violence issues.

To be homeless in San Francisco, living off the labor of the other residents, is quite a good deal. With over $600 per month, shelter, free transportation, food assistance of nearly $200 per month, and basic medical insurance, what more does anyone need? It is not farfetched to suggest that completely severing all of these programs would yield a

Covered in Fecal Matter". *Townhall*.

7   Knight, Heather. (June 26, 2017). "Despite Money and Effort, Homelessness in SF as Bad As Ever". *San Francisco Chronicle*.

substantial decrease in the homeless population. If these programs were eliminated nationwide, the homeless population would be required to either utilize private charities in order to get back on their feet, or they would likely perish. Some may call this heartless, but for the same reason one does not feed wild animals in national parks, redistributing the fruits of another's labor only demotivates the laziest in society, who become dependent entirely upon the producers. It then demotivates the producers, as they begin to see no purpose in their labor, save for it subsidizing those who wish to abstain from labor. Eventually, that system will reach a tipping point where the lazy will outnumber the producers, and the entire economy will collapse under its own weight.

This is by no means the only example of socialist redistribution in the United States. Every state does this in some capacity or another, and the federal government also does it in egregious amounts. In 2019, the U.S. federal government redistributed over 72% of the $3.46 trillion in revenue it took[8] in the forms of $1.24 *trillion* in Medicare and Medicaid, $893.4 billion for Social Security, and $361.5 billion for food, housing, and other family assistance programs. This racks up to nearly $2.5 trillion ($2,494,900,000,000 to be nearly exact).[9] Had this copious amount of redistribution not happened at all, the $984.2 billion deficit the state ran in 2019 would have turned into a $1.512 *trillion* surplus (assuming no changes to revenue). To break even at the federal level, they could eliminate both the Social Security and corporate income taxes entirely, and it would still yield a $3.7 billion surplus.[10]

Not only would ending the welfare state be a restoration of property rights for the producers, but if the state refused even to collect the tax dollars that would otherwise be spent on these programs, it would have a substantial positive effect on the community as a whole. Going

---

8 "FY22 Federal Budget Revenue Actuals for Fiscal Years 2015 - 2019" Retrieved from https://www.usgovernmentrevenue.com/federal_budget_actual on October 21, 2020.

9 "FY22 Federal Budget Spending Actuals for Fiscal Years 2015 - 2019" Retrieved from https://www.usgovernmentspending.com/federal_budget_actual on October 21, 2020.

10 Based on FY19 Revenue Individual Income Tax - $1,717.9; Corporate Income Tax - $230.2; Social Security - $1,243.4.

back to the example of San Francisco, while the $275 million that the city redistributed makes up nearly two-thirds of their aid assistance spending, it is actually quite a small portion of their $9.7 billion spending budget (about 2.8%; 4.3% of all aid assistance).[11] That said, property owners in San Francisco could save an average of nearly $2,900 per year just in property taxes if the city would slash the $275 million in redistribution entirely. If the whole $415 million in aid assistance spending was slashed, this would save property owners over $4,300 per year.[12]

This, of course, is not to endorse the idea of property tax. In all actuality, property tax, or "ad valorem tax," as legislators like to call it, is a huge threat to property rights, and would make the likes of Karl Marx proud. With the existence of property tax, the end result is that no one ever actually owns their property. Sure, you may pay off the mortgage and have the deed in hand, but should you choose to stop paying the state their annual property tax, your property will be seized. Similarly to how a landlord can evict a tenant for nonpayment, the state's indefinite taxation of property means that in practice, you are just renting that property from them.

The most disgusting part of property tax is just how accepted it is in every corner of the United States. Every single municipality in every State levies a property tax of some percentage (currently ranging in average from 0.27% in Hawaii to 2.47% in New Jersey).[13] These taxes are levied against you based on how the local appraisal district values your property, which is ultimately an arbitrary number. Free market principles dictate that while there may be a market value for a particular commodity, the market value is entirely dependent upon actual sales. While it is easy to track the value of some commodities, such as corn, wheat, oil, soybeans, etc. due to their consistent daily sales in the marketplace, a plot

---

11 City and County of San Francisco Budget and Appropriation Ordinance. FY 2017-2018. Retrieved from https://sfcontroller.org/sites/default/files/Documents/Budget/FY17%20&%20FY18%20AAO%20FINAL%20Budget%20with%20tails.pdf
12 Based on San Francisco's current median home price of $1.61 million and current property tax rate of 1.188%. Reducing the $1.842 billion in property tax revenue by $275 million or $425 million would reduce property tax rate to 1.011% and 0.920% respectively.
13 Kiernan, John S. (February 25, 2020). "Property Tax by State". WalletHub.

of land is entirely unique to the rest of the market, especially if it has a structure on it. A 10-acre plot of land out in west Texas will sell for far less than a 10-acre plot in the Texas hill country. This is because most people see a higher value if land has unique natural landscape with trees, ponds, and fertile soil when compared to a flat desert landscape. Unlike most other commodities, no two plots of land are created equally, and therefore the value cannot truly be determined until it is sold at a price mutually agreed upon by the buyer and seller.

The appraisal district can arbitrarily tell a property owner that their property is worth $190,000 year-after-year, but if it only sells for $170,000, then the value of the property was $20,000 less than the state said it was. The end result is that the property owner overpaid their taxes every year and will never be refunded. Even if local governments implemented a policy that ended property tax on a homeowner once their mortgage was paid off and the deed was in their hand, the entire system is still fundamentally flawed. The amount of taxes assessed by the appraisal district is always an arbitrary guess. The city in which you live may say that your property tax rate is 1.335%, but until you sell your property, the appraisal district has no way of actually knowing its value in order to adequately assess the tax rate.

The real problem is that municipal and county governments love property tax because it is their biggest revenue generator, even in places like New York City, where the municipal government also collects its own income tax. With current property tax systems, it is impossible to know exactly what one's true valuation is. The only way to make a property tax system utilize a non-arbitrary number, and allow for the property to actually be owned by the property owner, would be to fix the rate based on the value at the time of purchase and end the taxation when the mortgage is paid off. This, of course, carries its own complications.

This system would effectively turn property tax into sales tax, and a steep one at that. A property bought for $200,000 in a municipality with a 1.5% annual property tax rate would have an effective sales tax rate of 45% over the life of a 30 year mortgage.[14] I make this point, not

---

14 Based on 1.5% of $200,000 for 30 years. $200,000 x 0.015 = $3,000/yr. $3,000 x 30 years = $90,000. $90,000 / $200,000 = 0.45 = 45%.

to endorse it as an idea to be adopted, but to expose exactly why local governments lust after the idea of property tax. It is a cash cow for them, and a never-ending one at that. Mortgage lenders make even more of a killing on property sales, but at least their collection of interest is warranted as they are the ones funding the initial purchase at a mutually agreed upon rate of interest. Their collection of interest also ends when you finish paying off the mortgage, and the interest is based upon the existing principle of the loan, and not an arbitrary value set by a statist bureaucrat every year.

When you actually break it down to its foundational components, the state's entire purpose when it comes to property tax (or any tax for that matter) is to take from the property owner, under threat of force, an arbitrary extortion fee. If the state intended it to be fair, they wouldn't use smoke and mirrors in order to con its citizens into thinking a 1.5% ad valorem tax is a good deal for them. As the old adage goes, the devil is in the details. Imagine for a moment the state treating property tax the same way they treat sales tax. The State of Texas currently levies a 6.25% sales tax, and grants local governments the authority to enact their own sales taxes, which are capped at 2%. This makes the highest sales tax rate in the state 8.25%. If that same $200,000 property was levied an 8.25% sales tax as opposed to a 1.5% annual property tax, the property owner would pay a total of $16,500 in sales tax, as opposed to $90,000 over the course of a 30-year mortgage (assuming the end of taxation after mortgage repayment is complete, and no variation of appraisal value). This would make an effective property tax rate of 0.275%. Of course, property tax continues to be collected even after the loans are paid off, making it infinitely worse. As stated earlier, you will never really own your property as long as the property tax system continues to exist.

This, sadly, is not the only way that the state infringes on property rights. As owners of property, we have, by natural right, the ultimate say in how that property is handled, and that includes the right to deny state agents, or anyone else for that matter, the ability to search, seize, trespass on our property, or perform any other act we as the property owner do not wish to allow. Unfortunately, there are over 2.3 million unwarranted and unreasonable searches of private property conducted every single day at airports across the United States, all of which require a mandated search of personal property by law prior to boarding. This is by no means the only method whereby illicit searches go on, but it is the one that happens the most often.

In 2017, there were 849.3 million searches in U.S. airports, all of which were conducted for the sole "reason" of individuals wanting to fly commercially as a means of transportation.[15] In the name of "national security," we have willfully allowed a part of our natural property rights to be trampled upon by tolerating the state's self-granted authority to search our baggage, ban certain properties, and scan our bodies in search of "dangerous" items. Of course, contrary to the very "national security" idea on which the Transportation Security Administration was created, they hold an impressive failure rate at detecting these items. In an article from *ABC News*, a guess of an 80% failure rate was "in the ballpark" according to sources they asked at the Department of Homeland Security.[16] This, however, is likely a conservative guess as in 2015, the then-acting head of the TSA, Melvin Carraway, resigned following the release of an Inspector General's report showing a 95% failure rate for the agency.[17]

The truth of the matter, however, is that being the victim of a terrorist attack or airline hijacking is incredibly rare, even before the time airport security was mandated by law. The following headline from Vox would lead any average person to believe that before the United States adopted mandatory airport security, hijackings were such a regular part of the airline industry that the state simply had to step in and fix it. The headline reads: "The U.S. once had more than 130 hijackings in 4 years. Here's why they finally stopped." In the article, the author begins by talking about the March 29th, 2016 hijacking of EgyptAir Flight 181. She then goes on to explain that between 1968 and 1972, airlines

---

15 Bureau of Transportation Statistics. https://www.bts.dot.gov/newsroom/2017-annual-and-december-us-airline-traffic-data Retrieved on July 30, 2018.

16 Kerley, David; Cook, Jeffrey. (November 9, 2017). "TSA Fails Most Tests in Latest Undercover Operation at US Airports". *ABC News*.

17 Costello, Tom; Johnson, Alex. (June 1, 2015). "TSA Chief Out After Agents Fail 95 Percent of Airport Breech Tests". *NBC News*.

departing in the United States had over 130 aircraft hijacked in order to conclude to the reader that the federal government mandating security checkpoints was the fix.[18]

While 130 hijackings in 4 years certainly sounds like a lot (about 33 aircraft per year), and it is a lot from a purely relative standpoint, when you compare that to the 5.1 million airline departures from 1970 alone, the 33 aircraft hijackings translates to 0.0006% (that is six ten-thousandths of one percent) of flights. To be clear, this 5.1 million number is based on worldwide airport departures of airlines registered with the United States, but seeing as how the nation with the 2nd most worldwide departures that year was Germany with 1.15 million (merely 22% of the 5.1 million departures of U.S.-registered airlines), it is safe to conclude that a substantial majority of the U.S. registered departures were departures from within the U.S.[19] If it happened to be a 50% split of U.S. registered departures originated from within the U.S., then the 33 flights that were hijacked in 1970 amounts to 0.0013% of total flights.

While this is certainly not to downplay the trauma that victims of an airline hijacking go through, it is to show just how rare it was during the peak of airline hijackings in American history. The state's solution was to mandate that airline companies were to contract private airport security by law and require the searching all passengers and luggage for weapons and other contraband prior to boarding. Following the terrorist attack on the World Trade Center and the Pentagon on September 11, 2001, that contractual mandate turned into searches conducted by the state itself. This decision obliterated the natural right to one's property, trading it for the illusion of security at the airport. It is merely an illusion because not only do they fail the overwhelming majority of audits performed, but even should they find a weapon, there is no way to prove the individual had malicious intent to use the weapon on the flight. Carrying a handgun, knife, or other weapon in and of itself does not prove, nor is

---

18 Nelson, Libby. (March 29, 2016). "The US Once Had More Than 130 Hijackings in 4 Years. Here's Why They Finally Stopped". *Vox*.
19 "Registered Carrier Departures Worldwide". http://www.nationmaster.com/country-info/stats/Transport/Air-transport/Registered-carrier-departures-worldwide#1970. Retrieved on August 6, 2018.

it indicative of, the individual's intent to use it maliciously. It could be for an infinite number of reasons that are ultimately the business of the individual himself. The fact that the TSA fails over 80% of tests to detect these "dangerous items" should not surprise anyone, and it should cause everyone to demand the agency be dissolved.

What is completely ironic, however, is that if airline companies enacted the exact same policies regarding security, but did so purely of their own free will (without any state mandate whatsoever), it would not be an infringement on our property rights. Because the right to property secures individual sovereignty, a property owner has an indisputable authority over all who enter. This means that companies like Delta Airlines could institute policies forbidding firearms, knives, and the incredibly dangerous liquids in bottles over 3 fluid ounces, and it would be fully within their power as the owner and operator of the aircraft to do so. They even have the power to mandate screenings of all passengers prior to boarding. The state, however, does not have this authority because the state is incapable of any property ownership. Property that we have been conditioned to believe as belonging to the state is, in all actuality, unowned by anyone, and therefore the individual has not only the right to be on "public property," but also the right to bear any personal property he desires while there.

The only time agents of the state actually have the authority to search personal property is at the expressed consent of the property owner. This holds true for any other individual as well, so the status of the person being an agent of the state is completely irrelevant. Agents of the state should not be placed in a station superior to the individual. This means that searches of any person or their property are only warranted if the individual to be searched consents to the search to be performed. Many might object to this on the grounds that accused criminals will have the ability to deny law enforcement the ability to search for evidence that, if found, would result in his conviction. The problem with this objection is that it ignores logic and the presumption of innocence. If a person has not been convicted of a crime, then he is to be presumed innocent of committing such an act. I will expound on this subject in a later chapter, but suffice it to say for the time being that invading the property rights of a person presumed to be innocent of a crime is logically the exact same as invading the property rights of a person proven to be innocent.

In the United States, search warrants are supposedly a means of protecting property rights, as they are only to be issued by a sitting judge after law enforcement officials have justly explained their case for probable cause. This, however, has been proven countless times to be ineffective in doing so. Not only are law enforcement officials capable of lying, just as any of us are, but judges have been known to issue warrants with very little convincing. Take as an example the facts surrounding the death of Breonna Taylor. Ms. Taylor's ex-boyfriend, Jamarcus Glover, had been under surveillance by the Louisville Metro Police Department for suspicion of drug trafficking. On the warrant the LMPD obtained to breach Ms. Taylor's apartment (an address at which Mr. Glover did not reside), the overwhelming majority of points listed as justification for the warrant had nothing to do with Ms. Taylor or her address. Only four of the 13 points listed on the warrant had anything to do with Ms. Taylor or her property. To summarize these four points, they were: [20]

1. On January 16, 2020, Mr. Glover was witnessed walking into Ms. Taylor's apartment, then leaving a short time later with a box,
2. A U.S. Postal Inspector confirmed that Mr. Glover had been receiving packages thought to contain narcotics at Ms. Taylor's address,
3. Ms. Taylor's vehicle had been spotted at Mr. Glover's address "on different occasions," and
4. A point simply stating what Ms. Taylor's address was.

It was later discovered that the biggest point of these four, the confirmation from the Postal Inspector, was a lie. On May 15, 2020, two days following Ms. Taylor's death at the hands of LMPD narcotics officers, the Louisville Postal Inspector, Tony Gooden told reporters at *WDRB News* that he had never spoken to LMPD officers regarding packages going

---

20 Affidavit for Search Warrant. (March 12, 2020). Retrieved from https://reason.com/wp-content/uploads/2020/06/Breonna-Taylor-search-warrants.pdf

to Ms. Taylor's address. Had he been approached by such an inquiry, he would have denied such affirmation, as he told the reporter there were "no packages of interest going there."[21] This means that LMPD narcotics officers obtained the warrant by falsification, and therefore her death was premised entirely on the presumed fact that her ex-boyfriend was seen picking up a package from her residence one time.

The warrant process, even if followed as per the strictest interpretation of the 4th Amendment of the United States Constitution, is not as ironclad as many believe it to be. In an op-ed written by criminal defense attorney Ted Shouse, he explains the process as he has witnessed it with his own eyes:

> *"The judge is supposed to read the application and ask questions to determine if probable cause exists. That's what the law requires for a judge to sign a search warrant.*
>
> *"In 21 years as a criminal defense attorney in Jefferson County I've seen this procedure dozens of times. Here's what that looks like: The police officers, always in plain clothes, appear unannounced in a courtroom. They linger until there is a break in the court's business. When a break occurs, they approach the judge and white noise is turned on to make their conversation inaudible to anyone else in the courtroom. A casual conversation happens, and the warrant is invariably signed.*
>
> *"The judge is not randomly assigned; the police can pick whichever judge they want. Believe me, if I could pick the judge in my cases, I would. The conversation between the police and the judge is not recorded. Nor is there a record of how these conversations came to happen."[22]*

Despite the massive flaws in the warrant process, sometimes the state will go out of its way to search or seize property without a warrant.

21 Riley, Jason; Green, Marcus; and Ragsdale, Travis. (May 16, 2020). "Louisville postal inspector: No 'packages of interest' at slain EMT Breonna Taylor's home". Retrieved from https://www.wdrb.com/in-depth/louisville-postal-inspector-no-packages-of-interest-at-slain-emt-breonna-taylor-s-home/article_f25bbc06-96e4-11ea-9371-97b341bd2866.html

22 Shouse, Ted. (June 22, 2020). "Opinion: Brionna's Law a Start, But Jefferson Circuit Court Should Change Warrant Process". *Courier Journal.*

Aside from cases where evidence is clearly fruit of the poisonous tree, there is massive, unwarranted seizures of personal property that happen every day in the United States. Similar to the TSA's bulk searches of air travelers, this atrocity affects every American; this is the mass collection of metadata. The question, of course, is whether or not conversations on a cell phone, text messages, emails, or even just the metadata of those are personal property. The answer is undoubtedly "yes."

Contained within our natural right to private property is our natural right to privacy. That is to say that if someone wants to lock themselves away from the world and become a recluse, it is his right to do so. Even if the entire population of the world were to demand him share his go-ings-on, be it out of fear, or mere curiosity, his ears should become deaf to these demands. Should he invite a friend inside, what takes place is purely the business of the two, and no one else. This principle, by extension, applies to any conversation we have with anyone else. We decide how public or private we want to be, and the warrantless collection of metadata by the National Security Agency is a gross invasion of our privacy, and therefore is a violation of our natural right to property. The collection of *anyone's* metadata should not occur without the person's consent under any circumstances, and no person would consent to such collection.

It is important to note that regarding privacy, we do not have the natural right to keep others from exposing our secrets if they happen upon a knowledge of them. If, for example, your neighbor overhears a phone conversation you are having in your back yard, you have no authority over what he does with the information he has obtained. If, on the other hand, he was to sneak onto your property and listen to a private conversation between you and your spouse, he has violated your property rights in order to obtain that information, and is therefore guilty of trespassing. While you still would not have authority over what he does with the information, as you have no authority over his mind and speech, his obtaining of that secret came as the result of criminal activity, of which he is guilty under the laws of nature.

To further explain this as it applies to the subject at hand, think of the warrantless collection of metadata as being no different from the collection of data about the mail delivered to your house. An agent of the state inspecting the specific contents of our mail would be an intrusion into our property, similar to how his listening in to our phone calls without our knowledge would be. What about if a state agency collected the weight, dimensions, date shipped, shipping company, and shipper information found on the label? If this were to happen to just one letter, then it might not worry the individual too much; but if it were to occur to every package, letter, catalogue, and magazine shipped to an individual's house, it would begin to tell a story about the recipient. A lot would be speculation, but some finer details would invariably emerge based solely on metadata about the mail delivered to their mailbox.

This is exactly what metadata is and why the NSA loves collecting it. Information about call duration, numbers called, text message length and time, data describing the color depth and resolution of images taken on a cell phone, the size of files on a computer, etc., all tell a unique story when pieced together. All of this is collected on millions of Americans every year, and all without a warrant. In 2017, the NSA collected 534 million call records, more than tripling its 2016 number of 151 million.[23] Probably the most interesting thing about this is that the number of people the NSA was actually targeting dropped from 42 to 40; meaning that if the Agency was purely gathering metadata from the targets alone, those targets would have had to conduct over 36,500 calls and text messages per day. This invariably means that the NSA is targeting an individual, and gathering metadata on everyone they have ever been in contact with.

The fact that the NSA even attempts to justify the warrantless collection of over half of a billion call records for the sake of targeting a few dozen people should be simultaneously laughable and infuriating. It should be laughable because it shows how inefficient the state is at doing anything; however, it should also be infuriating given the fact that not only do the resources that are dumped into this program rightfully belong to every individual who pays taxes to the federal government, but also that the program itself is being used to collect the data of the same people footing the bill in a vain attempt to stop a person with malicious

---

23 Coldewey, Devin. (May 4, 2018). "NSA Triples Metadata Collection Numbers, Sucking Up Over 500 Million Call Records in 2017". *TechCrunch.*

intent. Though it is classified, a leaked report from 1996 indicated that the NSA's budget was about 14% of the total intelligence budget that year.[24] Assuming no change in that figure, the NSA's 2017 budget was $10.2 billion of the total $73 billion intelligence budget.[25] It would be pure speculation to state just how much money was used to target 40 people and collect metadata on millions of Americans without a warrant, but seeing as how this is the main mission the NSA executes, it's likely that the majority of their budget funds metadata collection. Assuming just half of their budget goes to this program, American taxpayers paid $127.5 million per person targeted by the Agency, all while there is not enough evidence to even secure a warrant under our current system (rubber-stamped warrants included).

The very fact that the NSA is able to collect the metadata of Americans without a morsel of scrutiny is indicative of the amount of conditioning that the American people have had in believing that giving up essential liberties in order to purchase a little temporary safety is essential to the preservation of liberty itself. Sadly, this sort of foolish and misguided faith in the state has become the very reason Americans have lost so much liberty over the decades. The state has always been corrupt and inept in quite literally everything it does, and the amount of evidence to support this is so widespread that it is baffling just how many Americans continue to run to the state to solve all of their problems.

One of the most corrupt and egregious abuses of state power comes from the idea of eminent domain. Under this bogus power, the state has the authority to seize an individual's privately owned property for public use in order to benefit the population at-large. That is the theory behind it, anyway. Theory aside, this is by definition a communistic practice. In reality, eminent domain has been used habitually for public and private projects with a corrupt state ordering the seizure. As a result, people are forced by the state to give up their property against their will, and a supposed "fair market value" is paid to the owner. I had previously mentioned how a property's value is only truly determined at the point

---

24 Sahadi, Jeanne. (June 7, 2013). "What the NSA Costs Taxpayers". *CNN Money*.
25 U.S. Intelligence Community Budget. Retrieved from https://www.dni.gov/index.php/what-we-do/ic-budget on August 10, 2018.

of sale, but this is under the assumption that both the buyer and seller are in agreement with the price. In circumstances where eminent domain is claimed, the property owner has no real choice in the matter. He either accepts the check and vacates the property, or he faces a threat of violence by the state and his property is seized anyway.

Supporters of eminent domain love citing the Fifth Amendment of the United States Constitution, which states, in part, that, "private property [shall not] be taken for public use, without just compensation."[26] This, like so many other things, is never dissected beyond what lies on the surface. At face value, this is believed to be the end of the debate; the state has the power to seize property for public use so long as the property owner is compensated justly. This ultimately begs the question as to whether compensation is to be considered "just" if the owner does not agree to sell. Regardless of how the word "just" is defined in the Constitution is entirely beside the point. The Constitution is not the source of an individual's natural rights. The Constitution was meant to define the powers of the state, and the Bill of Rights was supposedly instituted to further protect an individual's natural rights by further limiting the powers of the state; it was not designed to grant us rights. Ultimately, it does not matter what the Constitution actually says. If our natural rights are infringed on by the state, then the state is guilty of tyranny. If the Founders actually intended for the federal government to have the power to seize property for public use against the will of the property owner and enshrined it in the Constitution, it is still a violation of our natural rights and should be rejected.

John Locke wrote extensively on the natural right of property, saying repeatedly that property was the fruit of our labor. As such, no one but the property owner has the right to dictate what happens with the property.

> *"The labour of [a man's] body, and the work of his hands, we may say, are properly his. Whatsoever then he removes out of the state that nature hath provided, and left it in, he hath mixed his labour with, and joined to it something that is his own, and thereby makes it his proper-*

---

26 United States Constitution. Amendment V.

ty. It being by him removed from the common state nature hath placed it in, it hath by this labour something annexed to it, that excludes the common right of other men: for this labour being the unquestionable property of the labourer..." [27]

Under this philosophy, there is zero doubt that eminent domain is a violation of the natural right to property. The only way property that is rightfully owned by an individual can be taken under Lockean principles is if the property is lying waste. Even under current law, an abandoned property can be claimed by anyone and property rights will be relinquished from the original owner. Of course, this has a lot of stipulations behind it that must be met in order to defeat a legal challenge from the original owner, but this sort of seizure is legal in the U.S., and rightfully so. This does not mean, however, that one must farm their land in order to claim ownership of it. Simply put, by keeping one's house cleaned and mowing the grass, a property owner mixes one's labor with the land, thus making it his property.

The acquiring of abandoned and neglected property is not the same as eminent domain, however. In what is likely to be a majority of eminent domain cases, property owners are forced to vacate their rightfully owned property against their will under threat of force. In one famous miscarriage of justice, the Supreme Court ruled in *Kelo v. City of New London* (2005) that the state's seizure of private property and the subsequent giving of it to another private entity for the purposes of spurring economic development satisfied the "public use" phrase of the Fifth Amendment's Takings Clause. In the Court's eyes, the City of New London, CT was perfectly within their authority in seizing private property because it was "projected to create in excess of 1,000 jobs, to increase tax and other revenues, and to revitalize an economically distressed city, including its downtown and waterfront areas," even though pharmaceutical giant, Pfizer, Inc., would gain ownership of the property. In the Opinion of the Court, Associate Justice John Paul Stevens wrote, "local planners hoped that Pfizer would draw

---

27 Locke, John. "Second Treatise of Government." Chapter V.

new business to the area, thereby serving as a catalyst to the area's rejuvenation... Just as we decline to second-guess the City's considered judgements about the efficacy of its development plan, we also decline to second-guess the City's determinations as to what lands it needs to acquire in order to effectuate the project."[28] This disgusting ruling has set the legal precedent that as long as a government can show that they planned to stimulate their economy in any way, even if they subsequently fail to do so, they can seize your property and gift it to a private corporation.

One thing that is separated from eminent domain, but is equally repugnant to liberty, is the idea of civil asset forfeiture. While eminent domain seizes people's homes and land, the one small positive is that the property owners are at least paid for their property (albeit not a fair value). With civil asset forfeiture, a person's assets are seized under the assumption of a crime having been committed, and those assets are later awarded to the seizing authority in civil court. This entire idea destroys the premise of innocent until proven guilty and violates property rights on the most direct level possible: outright theft.

Sadly, the same people who wrote the Fourth Amendment to protect the right of personal property from unwarranted seizure were the same to introduce asset forfeiture laws, though these early laws required criminal acts to be committed. During the First Congress of the United States, an act for *Regulation on the Collection of Duties on Tonnage and on Merchandise* established the first forfeiture law. This act mandated that "no goods, wares or merchandise, shall be unladen or delivered, from any ship or vessel, but in open day, or without a permit from the collector for that purpose." Violating this act incurred a $400 fine (over $11,800 in 2020)[29] for each person involved and "all goods, wares and merchandise, so landed or discharged, shall become forfeited, and may be seized by any officer of the customs."[30] This and subsequent acts were based on

---

28 *Kelo v. New London.* 545 U.S. 469 (2005). Retrieved from https://supreme.justia.com/cases/federal/us/545/469/
29 Based on calculations from https://www.officialdata.org/1789-dollars-in-2020?amount=400
30 *Regulation on the Collection of Duties on Tonnage and on Merchandise.* (1789). 1 Stat. 29. Retrieved from http://www.constitution.org/uslaw/sal/001_statutes_at_large.pdf

British maritime laws and were designed to aid in the collection of import tariffs, which, at the time, were responsible for nearly 90% of federal revenue generated.[31]

Today, asset forfeiture does not require a criminal charge in most states, and the burden of proof rests entirely on the owner of the seized property. To name one of countless examples, in 2018, a West Virginia State Trooper pulled over a man and his 8-month pregnant wife for failing to stay within his lane. During the stop, the Trooper accused the couple of smuggling cigarettes, possessing drugs, and gift card fraud. After searching the vehicle and their persons, the Trooper found $10,480 in cash, twenty-seven $100 gift cards, and fifty-one rewards program cards from various chain businesses. Finding no actual evidence of a criminal act, the Trooper wrote the driver a warning, but seized everything except $2 in cash. The driver's cell phone was also seized. After over 10 weeks of calling the State Police, the Jefferson County Prosecutor, and local politicians, all of their property was returned to them before it ever headed to civil court for forfeiture. Had it been forfeited, the non-liquid assets would have been sold, and 90% of the cash and proceeds from the sales would go to the seizing authority under West Virginia law. The remaining 10% would go to the prosecutor's office.[32]

This couple was extremely lucky. In most cases, assets that are seized end up in civil court, and it is up to the property owner to prove that the seizure was unwarranted. Because it is in civil court, the fact that no criminal charges were filed is irrelevant, and not a basis of dismissal. Winning back one's seized property is incredibly difficult, and because of the war on drugs and the existence of laws designed to combat money laundering, attempting to justify it with "it's my property and I can do with it what I want," is likely to result in forfeiture. Fighting asset forfeiture cases essentially requires the representation of an attorney, which can easily cost more than the property is worth, and in the end, it really is up to how the presiding judge feels that particular day.

---

31 Mellor, Chip. (June 8, 2011). "Civil Forfeiture Laws and the Continued Assault on Private Property". *Forbes.*

32 Zuckerman, Jake. (August 25, 2018). "WV State Police Seize $10k From Couple Without Charging Them With a Crime". *Charleston Gazette-Mail.*

Because of this, state authorities take advantage of asset forfeiture surprisingly often as it is basically free money for them. State and local agencies seem to love it almost as much as they love property tax. Depending on the State, the local law enforcement agency (including the district attorney) can keep the following percentage of the proceeds from the seized assets:

- 90–100% - 29 States plus the U.S. Federal Government.
  - AL, AZ, DE, GA, HI, ID, IA, KS, KY, MA, MI, MN, MT, NV, NH, NJ, ND, OH, OK, PA, RI, SC, SD, TN, UT, VA, WA, WV, and WY.
- 70–85% - 4 States.
  - AK, FL, LA, and MS.
- 45–69.5% - 7 States.
  - CA, CO, CT, NE, NY, OR, and VT.
- 0% - 7 States plus the District of Columbia.
  - IN, ME, MD, MO, NM, NC, and WI. [33]

While some States have enacted laws designed to curb the corruption that is invariably bred by asset forfeiture (or at least designed to give the illusion of doing so), it is still very rampant across the United States. Reforms on asset forfeiture have been lackluster at best and, in reality, have done far more to expand forfeiture than restrict it simply because the profit incentive is far too enticing to pass up. This is particularly true for agencies with tight budgets. In a scathing piece published in The New Yorker, author Sarah Stillman exposes multiple disgusting cases in which innocent people were victimized by their local governments and never charged with a crime:

> *"[C]ivil-forfeiture statutes continued to proliferate, and at the state and local level controls have often been lax. Many states, facing fiscal crises, have expanded the reach of their forfeiture statutes, and made it*

---

33 Carpenter II, Dick M., PhD; Knepper, Lisa; Erickson, Angela C.; McDonald, Jennifer. (November 2015). "Policing for Profit: The Abuse of Civil Asset Forfeiture 2nd Edition". *Institute for Justice.*

easier for law enforcement to use the revenue however they see fit. In some Texas counties, nearly forty per cent of police budgets comes from forfeiture." [34]

Even in States where the majority of proceeds goes to the State's general fund (or other State fund) instead of into law enforcement's coffers, there are easy ways to circumvent these measures, thanks in large part to the federal government. In 1984, Congress passed the Comprehensive Crime Control Act, which massively overhauled the federal criminal statutes. One new provision was to create what has become known as the Equitable Sharing program, which is overseen by the Department of Justice. This program allows States to circumvent their own restrictions when it comes to civil asset forfeiture, even in the 9 States that require a criminal conviction before assets can be seized. (These States are CA, MN, MO, MT, NV, NM, NC, OR, and VT.)

Here is how the Equitable Sharing program works using a hypothetical scenario: a Las Vegas police officer pulls over a car for a busted tail light and discovers $10,000 in cash. He cannot find any evidence of an actual crime, so he writes the driver a citation for the tail light, seizes all of his cash (citing he suspects it to be drug related), and lets the driver go on his way. The officer then logs the cash into the department. Because Nevada law requires a criminal conviction before assets can be forfeit, filing a civil forfeiture case in Nevada courts will result in restoration of the property to the property owner. The LVPD circumvents this hurdle by turning the seized cash over to the U.S. Drug Enforcement Administration, again citing the belief that it was drug related. The DEA files a civil forfeiture case for the $10,000 in federal court and the case *United States v. $10,000* is born. (This is legitimately what the case would be named in this scenario.) Once the judge presiding over the case rules in favor of forfeiture, the Equitable Sharing program shares the proceeds of the cash. In most cases, up to 80% of the proceeds goes to the local law enforcement agency and 20% goes to the DEA. As a result, the Las Vegas Police Department in this scenario essentially stole

---

34 Stillman, Sarah. (August 12, 2013). "Taken". *The New Yorker.*

$10,000 from an innocent man, and paid the federal government 20% to launder it for them.

The Equitable Sharing program is also used in States where they would have no problems keeping it at the State level, though typically, the biggest participants in the program are States with the strictest forfeiture regulations and burdens of proof. There is, of course, an exception to this rule. According to the previously cited *Institute for Justice* report (footnote 33), Texas has incredibly lax standards for asset forfeiture, and law enforcement agencies are awarded 70% of forfeiture proceeds (unless the property owner contests the forfeiture and loses, in which case the agency is awarded 100%). On its own, the Lone Star State was awarded nearly $63 million in forfeiture proceeds in 2013, but Texas was also the recipient of nearly $34 million in Equitable Sharing proceeds.

On the opposite side of the spectrum, New Mexico recently adopted incredibly strict regulations, effectively eliminating civil asset forfeiture altogether. For assets to become forfeit, the property owner must be charged with and convicted of a crime, and the property must be directly tied to that crime. The reforms also effectively banned law enforcement agencies from participating in the Equitable Sharing program. According to the *IJ* report:

> *"New Mexico's 2015 reforms prohibit law enforcement from transferring property worth less than $50,000 to the federal government for forfeiture and require that all proceeds be deposited in the state's general fund. This rule effectively disqualifies New Mexico from participating in federal equitable sharing since DOJ guidelines require that equitable sharing funds be spent solely by law enforcement on law enforcement purposes."*

New Mexico stands alone in this regard, unfortunately. No other state has adopted reforms that close the gaping loophole created by the Equitable Sharing program. This incentivizes agencies in strict-forfeiture states to use it, as they are all reluctant to willingly forfeit their cash cow. That said, New Mexico's new reforms still violate property rights.

As has been said numerous times, no person or entity besides the owner of the property has the right to lay claim to it. Any act of doing so is by its very definition "theft." John Locke explained it perfectly well in the quote that opened this chapter "Whenever legislators endeavor to take away and destroy the property of the people... they put themselves in a state of war with the people, who are thereupon absolved from any further obedience." Ultimately, it does not matter if the property was acquired as the result of what is considered a criminal act (unless that criminal act itself was theft, in which case the property would be returned to the rightful owner and not forfeit to the state). It is a violation of a property owner's rights to seize private property that rightfully belongs to a person suspected, or even convicted of a crime. It is still rightfully their property.

The state's recognition of property rights is absolutely nonexistent. For over a century, property rights have been trampled on by the state in so many ways that it would be impossible to lay out every method in a single chapter. Additional property infringements will be discussed in subsequent chapters, but even those will not be a complete list. Many people seem to be reluctant to end most, if not all, of these programs because statism has conditioned them to believe them necessary. Any time programs like Social Security or welfare are brought up in political debates, the media conveys the message that those who even bat an eye at the program must hate senior citizens or poor people. These cut and paste stories lead good people to believe that ending food stamps will cause millions of Americans to starve to death and become homeless, that without the TSA or NSA spying, terrorist attacks will become common place on American soil, and without property taxes, public schools will end and children will become imbeciles. When boiled down to its base components, the common person has been conditioned to believe that without the state's involvement and control in x then epidemic y will result. When those arguments come up short, then we are to think of the children.

We should want our children to live in a society where individual liberty is championed and where their right to property is unquestioned. We are raised being taught that theft is bad, yet we tolerate it when the state does it in the name of charity, security, and justice. These are all lies. Redistribution of wealth is not charity, nor is it charitable. Charity is giving to those in need, and doing so voluntarily is the act of being charitable. Since taxation is taken (not given) under threat of force, it fits neither definition. Eliminating all of these socialist programs would do wonders for the world. We would all become far more charitable in our actions. It would be up to us to take care of the less fortunate in our community, and we would feel a responsibility help lift them up. The less fortunate would end up being actually given a hand up out of poverty instead of having their problems perpetuated by the state. In the end, the less fortunate would be able to pull themselves up and prosper, making everything better as a result.

Programs that the state uses to usurp our rights need to end immediately. The doomsday scenarios of constant terrorist attacks that we are warned about would not come to fruition. Ending the TSA and all airport security mandates would drive airlines to come up with their own security measures, should the market demand them. These would likely develop in such a way as to not only be less invasive for consumers, but also more secure for the airlines themselves. Profit incentive is a powerful thing, and turning the security measures of their airline into a selling point would be a cause for competition in the market, which always yields a better product.

The state's unwarranted collection of data or property needs to be abolished as well. The NSA's program specifically has prevented exactly zero terrorist attacks from happening on American soil, and costs taxpayers billions of dollars every year.[35] Asset forfeiture programs do nothing to deter crime because no crime needs to even be proven to have been committed in most cases. It is a funding tool for law enforcement that is literally theft from private individuals, and eminent domain carries the same result. None of these programs benefits the individual in any way, but they do have a detrimental effect on their victims.

---

35 Isikoff, Michael. (November 2, 2015). "NSA Program Stopped No Terror Attacks, Says White House Panel Member". *NBC News*.

Chapter 3

Taxation is Not Theft...
It is Extortion

"There is no worse tyranny than to force a man to pay for what he does not want merely because you think it would be good for him."
- Robert A. Heinlein

In an adage nearly everyone knows, Benjamin Franklin was quoted as saying, "Nothing can be said to be certain, except death and taxes." History has proven him right, but the extent to which it has done so has gone far beyond what the patriots of 1776 ever could have anticipated. Taxation is a cancer of the modern era. The most disturbing symptom is that a majority of good and honest Americans have become complacent in, or even blind to the fact that the U.S. federal government extorts a sizable percentage of their earnings each and every year. They justify this blatant and ungodly amount of extortion by parroting the same talking points fed to them by elite politicians:

- *"Taxes are the price we pay to live in a civilized society."*
- *"Without taxation, what will become of the roads and bridges?"*
- *"We need taxes to pay for basic services like firefighters and police!"*

The problem, of course, is that this is nothing more than propaganda. Given that the fiscal policy of the state is about as intriguing as a thesis on the total nitrogen retention in fecal matter, most Americans tend to not care about it at all. In fact, taxation, or even fiscal policy generally, was nowhere to be found among the most important issues facing voters in the 2016 Presidential Election. The economy was the top issue, according to *Forbes*, followed by terrorism, foreign policy, healthcare, and gun policy.

At the bottom of *Forbes'* top 14 list was "treatment of LGBT people" with 40% reporting it as a "very important" issue for them.[36]

The present state of affairs is sad, and incredibly ironic, when one realizes that the biggest issue sweeping the American colonies in the late 1760s and early 1770s was taxation on imported tea. While it is true that the first shots were fired at Lexington and Concord due to the British Army mobilizing to seize or destroy the colonists' arms, all of the political turmoil that had led up to that point stemmed from the colonists' grievances of having taxes levied on them by the Crown without any representation in Parliament.

Following the Seven Years' War, the British Crown had undertaken massive debt in order to fund their war efforts. As a result, King George III's Parliament enacted the Sugar Act of 1764. This act reduced the import tariffs on sugar, molasses, and syrups, but simultaneously strengthened enforcement measures that colonists had evaded for thirty years.[37] The King had hoped that despite the tax rate being reduced from six pence to three pence per gallon, the more stringent enforcement mechanisms for collecting import duties would actually yield more revenue to the Crown.

Ultimately, this was the first of many taxing acts to cause discussion in the American Colonies. With the Tea Act of 1773, Parliament sought to bail out the East India Company (which was going bankrupt despite having a monopoly on all tea imports into the colonies) by levying a three pence tax for every pound of tea imported. This was essentially no different than the 2009 bailout of General Motors. Unlike corporate bailouts of today, the colonists protested the Tea Act by holding tea parties in Boston, Philadelphia, Charleston, and other cities along the coast, destroying the tea by either burning it or tossing it into the harbor. During the Boston Tea Party alone, the Sons of Liberty destroyed 92,000 pounds of tea that the East India Company valued at £9,659 (or over $1.7 million today).[38]

---

36 McCarthy, Niall. (July 11, 2016). "The Top Issues For Voters in the 2016 Presidential Election [Infographic]". *Forbes*.
37 Dickerson, Oliver M. (1951). *The Navigation Acts and the American Revolution*.
38 The Boston Tea Party Museum. "The Destruction of the Tea." Retrieved from https://www.bostonteapartyship.com/the-destruction-of-the-tea on October 29, 2018.

What is really interesting is just how little of a tax the Tea Act implemented relative to today. The 92,000 pounds of tea valued at £9,659 puts each pound of tea worth about 2 shillings (notated £0.10) before the tax. Under the old pound, shilling, pence system, there were 12 pence to a shilling and 240 pence to £1. Adding 3 pence to 2 shillings puts the amount cost at £0.1125 per pound of tea after tax, or an effective tax rate of just 12.5%. To translate this even further, the Sons of Liberty rebelled against the King in an extraordinary and historic manner for increasing the price of tea from about $17.76 to $19.99 per pound in today's currency.[39]

While this tax was an import tariff and not a sales tax, it is important to note that tariffs were the main revenue-generator of the time. There were no personal income, corporate income, or payroll taxes in existence. This means that comparing the 12.5% tariff levied by the Tea Act to today's weighted mean tariff rate of 1.67% is not exactly apples-to-apples.[40]

Following the creation of the United States Constitution in 1787, taxation was not practiced much differently. In 1802 under President Thomas Jefferson, the national revenue was $15.3 million ($361 million in 2018), 94% of which was generated from import duties and fees.[41] It wasn't until 1861 that Congress actually passed the first income tax to help fund the Union's war efforts. The Revenue Act of 1861 exempted 97% of Americans from the income tax, as it only applied a 3% tax to incomes over $800 ($20,000 in 2018). It was ultimately never levied as Congress attempted to make it more comprehensive with the Revenue Act of 1862, which was again revised in the Revenue Act of 1864.[42] The 1864 Act ultimately expired in 1873, during which over 88% of the revenue generated was still from import duties and sources other than

---

39 Based off the proportions that (£0.10/£9,656)=(x/$1,700,000) and (£0.1125/£9,659)= (y/$1,700,000).

40 "Tariff Rate, Applied, Weighted Mean, All Products (%)". *World Bank Group.* Retrieved from https://data.worldbank.org/indicator/TM.TAX.MRCH.WM.AR. ZS?locations=US on October 29, 2018.

41 "United States Federal Revenue, Fiscal Year 1802". Retrieved from https://www. usgovernmentrevenue.com/year_download_1802USmn_20ms1n_61E1#usgs302 on November 4, 2018.

42 Nisbet, Jack and Claire. (September 14, 2011). "President Abraham Lincoln Signs the Revenue Act, Which Includes the First Federal Income Tax, on August 5, 1961". *HistoryLink.*

income.[43] The United States would not see another income tax until the Wilson-Gorman Tariff Act of 1894, but this was struck down by the Supreme Court a year later in *Pollock v. Farmers' Loan & Trust Co.*[44]

The income tax we all know and love today was first instituted in one massive move that grew the size of the federal government to unprecedented levels in 1913. In February of that year, the 16th Amendment was officially ratified, nullifying the *Pollock* decision, and making income tax legal. In October, President Woodrow Wilson signed the Revenue Act, and on December 23, he signed the Federal Reserve Act. Not only did the year 1913 see the legalization and institution of a tax directly on the fruits of one's labor, but it also saw the creation of the most destructive entity ever conceived to oversee the value of every American's hard-earned dollar (and subsequently destroy it): the Federal Reserve System. The Fed, however, is an abomination best left to be expounded upon in its own chapter.

Over the last century since the institution of a legalized income tax, the top tax rates have fluctuated from as little as 7% on incomes over $500,000 in 1913 ($13.1 million in 2020) to 94% on incomes over $200,000 in 1944 ($3.0 million in 2020).[45] Currently, the top tax rate is 37% on incomes over $500,000 (down from 39.6% of $418,400 in 2017) after President Donald Trump signed the Tax Cuts and Jobs Act (though this act expires in 2025).[46] As a result of the massive growth of government in 1913, nearly 56% of the federal government's revenue in 2017 was generated by income tax alone (nearly 92% if you include the Social Security tax).[47]

While income tax is the single biggest revenue generator for the federal government, and is the one tax that most Americans seem to care about, the pure volume of taxes that are levied against us all on a daily

43 "United States Federal Revenue, Fiscal Year 1872". Retrieved from https://www.usgovernmentrevenue.com/year_download_1872USmn_20ms1n_E1404146#usgs302 on November 4, 2018.
44 *Pollock v. Farmers' Loan & Trust Co.* 157 U.S. 429 (1895). Retrieved from https://supreme.justia.com/cases/federal/us/157/429/
45 "History of Federal Income Tax Rates: 1913-2018". *Bradford Tax Institute*. Retrieved from https://bradfordtaxinstitute.com/Free_Resources/Federal-Income-Tax-Rates.aspx
46 El-Sibaie, Amir. (January 2, 2018). "2018 Tax Brackets". *Tax Foundation*.
47 "United States Federal Revenue, Fiscal Year 2019". Retrieved from https://www.usgovernmentrevenue.com/year_download_2019USmn_20ms1n_1030#usgs302 on October 22, 2020.

basis should in and of itself be cause for alarm for everyone. In fact, there are more than a handful of taxes that we never see, as they are all rolled into the price of the products we purchase. Other taxes are called either "tariffs," "fees," or "licenses" by the state, but they are no different than taxation from a legal standpoint. Here is a heavily abridged list of the taxes we pay other than income tax:

- Property Tax
- Sales Tax
- Marriage License
- Gift Tax
- Air Transportation Tax
- Inheritance Tax
- Vehicle Inspection Fee
- Vehicle Registration Fee
- Garbage Collection Fee
- Firearm Carry License
- Liquor Tax
- Gasoline Tax
- Driver's License
- Pet License

In 2009, a phenomenon began sweeping the nation following the inauguration of President Barack Obama; an ideology of fiscal conservatism began forming what became known as the Tea Party movement. Just eight months after President Obama took office, a massive rally "in excess of 75,000" people was held in Washington D.C. to protest a myriad of big government habits, including the national debt (which was $13 trillion at the time), deficit spending, the state's intrusion in the free market, and President Obama's proposed Obamacare legislation.[48] The rapid growth of the movement caused Republican politicians to seek endorsements of local Tea Party organizations, and the revolutionary ideology adopted the "backronym" of "Taxed Enough Already."

---

48 Sherman, Jake. (September 13, 2009). "Protesters March on Washington". *The Wall Street Journal.*

This was definitely an exciting time to be a conservative Republican or even a libertarian. The movement seemed to be unstoppable, and the outpouring opposition to government spending poured over into the election of Republicans to Congress. The 2010 midterm elections saw Republicans gain 64 seats, giving them a sizable majority in the House of Representatives, and improving their minority in the Senate with a gain of 6 seats. The future of President Obama's agenda began looking bleak despite the signing of Obamacare into law in March of that year. With the power of the purse resting in the now Tea Party-controlled House, it seemed as if the ability to curtail out-of-control spending was attained, and the hemorrhaging would begin to stop.

This, unfortunately, proved to not be the case in 2011. In August of that year, the national debt ceiling was going to be hit. Unless Congress acted, the U.S. Treasury would not be able to borrow any more money to pay for budget items for which Congress had already committed the nation to pay. Politicians essentially said that raising the debt ceiling was needed to "pay the bills." In reality, this was a complete falsehood. When the average person "pays their bills," they have the cash to do so. What Congress was advocating for would equate to an individual increasing the credit limit on an already maxed-out credit card, and then using that to pay his car loan and electric bill.

Despite massive public opposition, the Republican-controlled House raised the debt ceiling by $900 billion to avoid default, the U.S. credit rating was downgraded from AAA to AA+ for the first time in history, and nothing actually changed from a fiscal standpoint. Again in 2013, 2014, 2015, and 2017, the debt ceiling was raised, and was ultimately suspended by President Trump on September 30, 2017.[49] This suspension grants the U.S. Treasury the authority to borrow as much money as required to "fulfill its obligations."

The truth of the matter is that despite all of the taxation that is taken from us each and every year, the U.S. federal government is flat broke. Here are some things to consider:

---

49 Lee, Frances. (September 10, 2017). "This is How Trump Turned the Politics of the Debt Ceiling Upside Down". *The Washington Post.*

- National Debt as of January 19, 2021 - $27.81 trillion[50]
- Federal Revenue, 2020 - $3.6448 trillion[51]
- Federal Spending, 2020 - $4.7456 trillion[52]
- Federal Deficit, 2020 - $1.1008 trillion
- Annual Interest on National Debt, 2020 - $478.8 billion
- Interest as a Percent of Federal Revenue – 13.1%

During the Obama administration, there was a graphic floating around social media that equated the fiscal policy of the U.S. government to the spending habits of a regular individual by removing just a few zeroes. Here is the updated version of that graphic:

- Current Debt - $278,100
- Annual Income - $36,448
- Annual Expenses - $47,456
- Current Deficit - $11,008
- Annual Interest - $4,478

If a loved one had $278,100 in debt and made just a little over $36,000 per year, yet spent nearly $47,500 every year, an intervention would be long overdue. It would be way past time for them to liquidate assets, slash *all* unnecessary spending, and destroy all of their credit cards. They certainly would not have a 770 credit rating from Experian, as their debt makes up 763% of their annual income.

Those who hold the libertarian philosophy often get hammered when they say, "taxation is theft," largely due to the fact that most people have been conditioned to believe in the necessity of taxation from the state. After all, we have never known a society without copious amounts of taxation, and therefore it is difficult for people to grasp the idea behind such a notion. As a result, the seriousness of this question never gets addressed. The question of whether or not taxation is necessary is a valid

---

50 Retrieved from www.usdebtclock.org.
51 "United States Federal Revenue, Fiscal Year 2019". Retrieved from https://www.usgovernmentrevenue.com/year_revenue_2020USbn_20bs1n on January 19, 2021.
52 "United States Federal Spending, Fiscal Year 2018". Retrieved from https://www.usgovernmentspending.com/year_spending_2020USbn_20bs2n on January 19, 2021.

one to dissect, and the discourse should be as serious as that on any other legitimate topic.

As expounded upon earlier, tariffs were the largest form of revenue generation for America all the way up until 1913. Tariffs are no different than any other tax, as they are a duty to be paid upon the importation of goods. No state in the history of the world has ever existed without taxation, but does that mean it is not theft? Dictionaries always seem to put an out in their definitions. For example, the Oxford English Dictionary includes the phrase "without legal right" in their definition of steal. Since it is the state that defines what constitutes "legal right," it seems on its face that taxation would, therefore, *not* be theft. This, however, defies logical sense.

If we delve into this deeper than just the surface we find something quite interesting. Reverting back to the last chapter regarding property, the question must be posed as to what point does an individual have the natural right to claim ownership of any property? In our current state of society, the default train of thought is that the voluntary exchange of money for goods or services constitutes a transfer of ownership of the property title. While this is certainly true, it neglects the keystone that is the epitome of property ownership.

It is an individual's *labor* that grants him the right to claim title of ownership over his property. In the state of nature, it is the growing of crops or the killing of game that entitles the farmer or the hunter to the right to lay claim of ownership over that which he has labored to produce. As its rightful owner, he can do with his property what he pleases. If both the farmer and hunter wish to hoard their property, then that is their right as the owners, just as it is their right to barter voluntarily x ears of corn in exchange for y pounds of meat. It is when an individual seeks to take possession of the farmer's crops or the hunter's kill without their consent that theft exists in the state of nature.

In today's state of society, the same holds true with a few variables. Instead of tilling fields and hunting game for sustenance, the vast majority of Americans voluntarily exchange their labor for currency by producing something for a business. One's labor is their property by definition, and since it is mutually agreed upon by the business owner and the laborer that he would exchange x hours of labor for y wages, this undoubtedly makes the laborer the owner of the currency paid to him. Using the basic scenario from the state of nature, the employee can choose to hoard his currency, should he so choose, or voluntarily exchange it for goods and services provided by others. It is an individual's seeking to take possession of the laborer's currency without their consent that constitutes theft in the state of society.

With this essential truth highlighted, we can now go back to the definition of "theft," and ask the necessary question: what grants the state the "legal right" under natural law to obtain possession of an arbitrary percentage of the fruits of one's labor? Many would usually attempt to answer this with one of the talking points listed at the beginning of this chapter, but none of them answers the fundamental question. Others might suggest the Thomas Hobbes view of a social contract, that essentially society has agreed to the taking of property to pay for the commonalities we enjoy, such as our roads and bridges. The fundamental problem with this philosophy is that, unless 100% of a population agrees with the form and rate of taxation, then anyone who dissents will have their natural rights violated, including anyone born thereafter.

Hobbes, in his 1651 work, *Leviathan*, cites the Bible as that which gives the state authority over taxation, but only to the extent that the people should pay their taxes due to them. Nowhere in this, arguably his most famous work, does he delve into what actually grants the state the right to claim ownership over the properties of the people, but he does say that the taxing authority should be equally placed upon the population at-large:

> *"To Equall Justice, appertaineth also the Equall imposition of Taxes; the equality whereof dependeth not on the Equality of riches, but on the Equality of the debt, that every man oweth to the Common-wealth for his defence."*[53]

Locke had a different approach to taxation, but nevertheless did justify its collection from the state. This justification was from a far more secular rationale than that of Hobbes, and Locke also said that it should be given the consent of the majority:

---

53 Hobbes, Thomas (1651). *"Leviathan"*. Equall Taxes.

"It is true, governments cannot be supported without great charge, and it is fit every one who enjoys his share of the protection, should pay out of his estate his proportion for the maintenance of it. But still it must be with his own consent, i.e. the consent of the majority, giving it either by themselves, or their representatives chosen by them: for if any one shall claim a power to lay and levy taxes on the people, by his own authority, and without such consent of the people, he thereby invades the fundamental law of property, and subverts the end of government."[54]

Locke's position is that he who enjoys the protection the state offers shall pay his portion for such protection is one that best explains the state's authority to tax, but it is still not without flaw. As previously stated, unless 100% of the population agrees, then each person who dissents must be coerced into the payment of the taxes levied against them. Failure to do so will result in the state placing the tax evader in a jail cell as punishment, and then seizing the taxes owed (plus interest). Should he refuse to be taken to the jail, state agents will be required to invoke violence against him, which will likely result in the tax evader's death; and in the eyes of the state, this is an appropriate use of force. This, by definition, means that taxation is not only theft, but is, more specifically, extortion.

Herein lies the conundrum. The state is in fact extorting monies from the people, under the inherent threat of violence for noncompliance, when it taxes them, regardless of the method of taxation implemented. Should someone refuse to pay the tax the state demands, there is no means by which the state can deny that individual the use of the public utilities to which those funds go, be it public roads, or even national defense in the form of a standing military. Proponents might justify taxation by stating that since the dissenting individual cannot be singled out when the state provides a social benefit to the population at-large, that individual is gaining a benefit from the state, while the rest of the population pays for it. In effect, they would conclude, it is this refusal to pay that is in and of itself a de facto form of theft. This, however, is by no means a valid argument.

---

54 Locke, John (1689). *"Second Treatise of Government"*. Chapter XI.

If, for example, Bob extorts $100,000 from John with a threat of violence for noncompliance, Bob is still the rightful owner of that $100,000. When the possession of the $100,000 changes from John to Bob, John did not transfer the title of ownership to Bob, as this can only be achieved through voluntary exchange. Because of the coercion from Bob's threat of violence against him, even though John chose to give Bob the money rather than face the consequences of noncompliance, his choice was not a free one to make, since self-preservation is in our nature.

Bob, now in possession of $100,000 rightfully owned by John, then goes to the Mercedes-Benz dealership and exchanges it for a brand new fully loaded AMG C63 Coupe, with a 4-year service package. The dealership, believing Bob to be the rightful owner of the $100,000, has not committed any wrongdoing, as it is not their responsibility to ensure title ownership of the funds used, but Bob has now committed the second criminal act of fraud. By using money extorted from John, and misrepresenting it as his property, Bob has defrauded the dealership out of one of their vehicles.

Now possessing the new Mercedes-Benz, Bob drives it back to John's house and eagerly hands him the keys and the title. There are two possibilities that could play out of this scenario. Whether or not John actually wants the car is entirely irrelevant. If John did want the car, then he would have made the purchase himself when he was ready to do so. If he did not want it, then what was given to him as a result of the extortion was something he would not have purchased himself, and he is now in possession of property he does not want. Either way, what Bob did violated John's property rights. By making the choice for John without his consent on how best to use his $100,000, Bob is guilty of theft. By using a threat of violence against him as a means of coercion, Bob is guilty of extortion. Finally, by transferring ownership of property that is not his to another party in exchange for goods, Bob is guilty of fraud. At no point in this scenario did Bob's actions magically transform from being criminal to moral, i.e., to being legitimate under the laws of nature. Likewise, at no point does the state's extortion from the individual become moral, even if the state provides a good or service in return. It is, and will always be, extortion.

As one final point, the logic surrounding the very premise of a social contract is nonexistent. Contracts by their very nature require consent from all parties to be considered valid. Even in today's state of society, courts will reject upholding any private contract in which one party was coerced into agreement. The glaring exception to this, however, is if the state brings charges against an individual for nonpayment of taxes. Despite no contract existing, be it physical or oral, the state jurists will always rule in favor of the state. The notion that one is subject to a contract by simple virtue of being born or residing in a geographic location is illogical. Certainly, you would reject any demands to fulfill terms of a private contract which was agreed to by another individual, even if that individual was a family member or friend. Unless you voluntarily cosigned the contract, you would not be responsible for its fulfillment.

To paint an extreme example of how a social contract works, imagine if Congress, duly elected by the people, passed an act requiring all adult citizens to have sex with either their Congressperson or one of their Senators. Even if such a repugnant provision were enshrined in the constitution, you would certainly find this to be unacceptable to say the absolute least. It would be rightfully proclaimed to be rape. Now let us assume that all people who identify with Political Party A agree with this new law, and only those who identify with Political Party B dissent. Does this change anything at all? Undoubtedly no. What if all 250 million American adults except for you agreed? The answer is still no. The state would have passed a law that would result in you being the victim of rape or subject to other violence for noncompliance. This holds true regardless of whether the entire population at-large agreed to it.

Under no circumstances should the notion of a social contract be considered valid, not for justifying taxation, nor for any other thing. A contract requires all parties involved to agree to its terms and conditions voluntarily and freely. Since no actual contract exists between the state and you as an individual stipulating that you will pay x percentage of your wages, y percentage of the value of the goods you purchase, or z percentage of an arbitrary valuation assigned to your property, the state has no authority to demand them from you, your children, or anyone of past, present, or future generations.

Chapter 4

Crony Capitalism

"I know of no example in time or place of a society that has been marked by a large measure of political freedom, and that has not also used something comparable to a free market to organize the bulk of economic activity."
– Milton Friedman

C apitalism is a beautiful thing, yet like liberty, is something that has not been seen in the United States for generations. Many Americans believe that the U.S. economy is capitalistic, and it is to some extent, but the overregulation, barriers to entry, and countless Federal and State laws prohibiting x, y, and z make the American economy a bastardized hybrid at best. I will try not to beat the property-rights horse to death any more than it already has been, but like the preceding two chapters, it is the very foundation of what makes an individual truly free.

There is so much that is wrong with the economic state of the United States that it actually perpetuates the political left's calls for the philosophy of rainbows and unicorns that is "democratic socialism." So many people who consider themselves pro-capitalist wonder how anyone with any sense can support the outlandish ideas put forth by open socialists like Senator Bernie Sanders or Congresswoman Alexandria Ocasio-Cortez. The answer, as asinine as it is, is quite simple: generations of people who have known nothing but *crony* capitalism are conditioned to believe it to be real capitalism, and therefore, are easier to brainwash against a truly free market system. In today's tech-heavy world (thank you, capitalism), the spread of both information and misinformation reaches countless people across the globe in a matter of seconds. When Karl Marx first published *The Communist Manifesto* in February of 1848, it could only be read by those who obtained one of the limited number of printed copies of it. Today, a single tweet can reach millions of people in a matter of hours and has the potential to reach everyone around the globe. Yes, even in today's crony capitalistic economy, great fortunes can be made from innovation, creativity, and invention, and despite the barriers that exist, they can be overcome. The problem is not the fact that we have something that resembles a free market; it is that we do not actually have a free market.

People who are flocking to the ideas of socialism do so because the effects of crony capitalism are actually represented in some of Marx's ideas, and when lies are rooted in bits of truth, they are easier to believe. Take this passage from Marx, for example:

> *"The bourgeoisie keeps more and more doing away with the scattered state of the population, of the means of production, and of property. It has agglomerated production, and has concentrated property in a few hands. The necessary consequence of this was political centralisation. Independent, or but loosely connected provinces, with separate interests, laws, governments and systems of taxation, became lumped into one nation, with one government, one code of laws, one national class-interest, one frontier and one customs-tariff."*[55]

If there is one thing on which the democratic socialists keep pouncing, it is big business. It is their belief that large corporations exploit the lower class by hoarding vast amounts of wealth, and thus are essentially robbing them of their ability to live a middle-class life. This is particularly persuasive when they can point out bits of truth to help perpetuate the bigger lie. A legitimate truth to persuade a student of socialism on the "evils" of capitalism would be how Amazon not only paid zero income tax in 2018, but also received a $129 million tax rebate from the federal government.[56] The law is supposed to apply equally to everyone, after all, so how can this be? This sort of revelation emotionally charges the student, and when one is hyper-focused with emotion, it is impossible for them to think logically.

---

55 Marx, Karl; Engles, Friedrich (February 1848). *The Communist Manifesto.* Chapter I
56 Stampler, Laura. (February 15, 2019). "Amazon Will Pay a Whopping $0 in Federal Taxes on $11.2 Billion Profits." *Fortune Magazine.*

The student can then move on to learn another emotionally-based half-truth about how the "greedy" CEO's of the mega-corporations make billions of dollars while their labor force struggles to make ends meet. In June of 2018, Senator Sanders lambasted the CEOs of Amazon, Walmart, McDonald's, and Disney, reflecting this very sentiment. In an interview with CNN, he said:

> *"It is beyond belief that a company like Disney, when they made $9 billion in profits last year, that you have working people [at Disneyland], who walk around, and they're in Donald Duck or Mickey Mouse costumes, or serve food, who literally don't have enough money to pay their rent."*[57]

From here, the rest of the false and completely illogical narrative is easy to sell without any substance whatsoever. When Amazon announced they would be opening a new corporate headquarters in Queens, New York, socialists like Congresswoman Ocasio-Cortez railed against the company. The truth was that a deal had been struck in which Amazon would get $3 billion in tax breaks, but still pay $27 billion over 25 years. Building the headquarters would have created anywhere between 25,000–40,000 jobs for the area (all of which would pay taxes to the city in the form of income and property taxes), and Amazon would invest billions in community improvement by default as well.[58] The narrative that Ocasio-Cortez perpetuated was that the city of Queens was actually going to give Amazon $3 billion in cash (not in the form of a tax break over 25 years), and the hatred spewing from her followers caused the company to cancel their plans to build there. Following the cancellation announcement, Ocasio-Cortez said, "I think it's incredible. I mean, it shows that everyday Americans still have the power to organize and fight for their communities and they can have more say in this country than the richest man in the world."[59]

57 Krieg, Gregory. (June 28, 2018). "Bernie Sanders is Hosting a Town Hall for Workers. Their CEOs are Invited". *CNN Politics.*
58 Kamisar, Ben. (February 17, 2019). "New York City Mayor de Blasio: Amazon 'Took Their Ball and Went Home'". *NBC News.*
59 *CBS News.* (February 14, 2019). "Alexandria Ocasio-Cortez Celebrates Amazon Move to Scrap New York Headquarters".

When you pair all of this with the promises of "free" stuff, such as health insurance or college, it is actually easy to see how people are brought to believe that socialism is a fairer system than capitalism. The problem is that these people are incapable of acknowledging the difference between capitalism and crony capitalism. As mentioned in chapter 3, acts that bail out corporations with tax dollars (or tax breaks), like King George attempting to bail out the East India Trading Company, is the very foundation of crony capitalism. It actually strips away the very things that make capitalism work.

The thing about the free market is that it does not have a safety net, and the notion that a company is too big to fail does not exist. A truly free market dictates that a company must thrive on their own merit, with an incentive to grow and be profitable. The basic rule is that failure to meet market demands will likely mean certain death for the company. If this was allowed to work in its pure form (meaning free from any and all state involvement), the market (aka the people) would be the single mechanism by which companies succeed or fail.

In truth, capitalism is a self-policing system, and that is what makes it beautiful. Take discrimination as a simple but extreme example of this. Let us pretend that Bob owns a small store in the suburbs, and he is a legitimately racist man who is an active member of his local Ku Klux Klan chapter. Under current law, if he were to put a sign out in front of his store that forbade entry of people of color and Jews, he would be sued and the state would essentially force him to shut his business down. While in theory this seems like a fantastic solution to deal with the absolutely disgusting mindset that he has, it has some unintended negative consequences.

First and foremost, it strips Bob of his right to exercise dominion over his property (as explained in chapter 2). It is important to remember that despite the fact that Bob is a deplorable human being, natural rights are not contingent on having good values. It also establishes the precedent that if anyone refuses to do business with anyone else, that the same can be applied, as was the case with the baker who refused to bake a cake for a wedding between two gay men who loved each other. Secondly, Bob will very much be aware of the legal consequences of putting up his sign, and he will likely not post it. The result will be that the market will be unaware of what type of person Bob is, and depending on the way he runs his store, he could be successful at it. The problem has not been solved.

Now pretend such anti-discrimination laws do not exist. It is quite likely that Bob will put up his sign, and the entire market will become acutely aware of his values (or lack thereof). The market can then respond by boycotts and social media campaigns shaming him for his views, and he will likely be out of business within a matter of weeks at the most. This approach requires exactly $0 in taxes being used to tie up the civil courts more than they already are, and it was the market, not the state, that put him out of business. In the best-case scenario for Bob, the backwards town in which he lives will respond positively to it, and Bob's store will run just fine; however, his success will be minimized as he could never truly grow beyond the borders of his town. Doing so would cause the rest of the market to respond negatively.

Since the logic behind this is simple and completely removed from emotional thinking, it can actually be applied to anything and everything a company does, from political donations to employee wages. To socialists, the "living wage" argument is rooted in their confusion that natural rights are equal to guarantees in life. Their belief is that we have a natural guarantee to a job that pays us enough to live on, and this argument fits nicely for someone at, or slightly above, minimum wage earnings. The reality with capitalism, though, is that it truly is fairer than any other economic system.

Labor is a commodity, just like any other thing. It is the individual who seeks to voluntarily exchange his labor and skills to the business owner for a wage agreed upon by both parties that determines the market value of his labor. Contrary to what seems to be common belief, the purpose of a business is to create capital and grow, not to employ anyone (though this is a natural byproduct of growth). An individual's wage is not determined by the amount of sweat wiped from his brow but by the actual value he produces for the company for which he works. Yes, it is labor intensive to don a Donald Duck costume in the 90° heat of a California summer in an effort to make crying children and exhausted parents smile, but that brings relatively minimal value to The Walt Disney Company compared to the value CEO Bob Iger brings by overseeing the entire company's operations and sales (despite the fact that he sits in an air-conditioned office). If their value were truly equal to the socialist's delight, then all 199,000 Walt Disney employees would have made a little over $45,125 in 2017.[60] This is, of course, under the assumption that all of the employees that would otherwise have made more for their skills elsewhere were perfectly content with devaluing themselves and their labor in order to bring up those that ultimately bring less value to the company.

Socialist ideas are particularly popular with young people likely due to the fact that since their marketable skill sets have yet to develop fully, the value they typically bring to a company is minimal. Teenagers who hold minimum wage jobs (federally $7.25 per hour as of this writing) see the surface argument in pushes for increasing the minimum wage to $15 per hour as a benefit to them with no consequence. Of course this is enticing because who would not want to more than double their wage at the stroke of the president's pen? Sadly, what is not truly realized is the negative unintended consequences of doing so.

As the business is the property of the owner, and every dollar the business generates is the fruits of his labor, he has the ultimate decision to hire someone at a mutually agreed upon wage. Once an agreement of wages in exchange for labor is reached, only then is the owner contractually obligated to the terms of that agreement and transfer what would otherwise be a portion of his property to the employee in the form of his wage. Wages are one of the biggest overhead costs that any business has, and should a business owner be forced by legislation to pay any wage above market value for a low-skill job, costs would have to be cut elsewhere to compensate. This means that should someone who owns a local hardware store with 15 full-time employees be forced to raise all of their wages from, for example, $8.50 per hour to a new minimum of $15 per hour, that would increase the owner's wage overhead from $265,200 per year to $468,000 without an increase in sales. To immediately compensate for this massive increase in overhead, the owner will have to either lay off 7 of his 15 employees ($262,080 annually), or cut all of his employee's hours from 40 per week to 22 hours

---

60 "The Walt Disney Company Reports Fourth Quarter And Full Year Earnings For Fiscal 2017" (Press Release). The Walt Disney Company. November 9, 2017.

per week ($257,400 annually).[61] Regardless of what he chooses, the employees will ultimately be the ones negatively affected.

The minimum wage is destructive by several other means as well, one of which should be at the forefront of economic thought. The minimum wage, though not intentionally so, is inherently racist (as are other laws that will be discussed later). In 1966, famed economist, Milton Friedman, penned an op-ed in *Newsweek* voicing his opposition to Congress' recent act to raise the federal minimum wage from $1.25 per hour to $1.60 per hour; his focus was on the racist impact these laws would have.

"The shockingly high rate of unemployment among teen-age Negro boys is largely a result of the present Federal minimum-wage rate. And unemployment will be boosted still higher by the rise just enacted. Before 1956, unemployment among Negro boys aged 14 to 19 was around 8 to 11 per cent, about the same as among white boys. Within two years after the legal minimum was raised from 75 cents to $1 an hour in 1956, unemployment among Negro boys shot up to 24 per cent and among white boys to 14 per cent."[62]

Dr. Friedman's op-ed was particularly concerned with black teenage unemployment and called the minimum wage law "the most anti-Negro law on our statute books—in its effect not its intent." Today, his concerns should be voiced even louder as the Bureau of Labor Statistics shows a fluctuation of black unemployment for ages 16 to 19 sits right at around 20% during the summer months with highs of nearly 30% in the springtime. Conversely, white unemployment for the same age group fluctuates slightly between 10–12% year-round.[63] The fact that there exists a major gap of skill sets between black and white teenagers is indeed troubling, however, it would be pure conjecture to speculate on the reason this gap exists. Dr. Friedman called it in his op-ed "a tragic but undoubted legacy of

---

61 Based off 15 or 8 full-time employees at $15/hr, 40 hrs/wk or 22 hrs/wk, 52 wks/yr. Excludes other overhead costs associated with hiring employees, such as payroll taxes, insurance, and/or other benefits.
62 Friedman, Milton (September 26, 1966). "Minimum-Wage Rates". *Newsweek*.
63 "Employment Situation." Table A-2. *Employment Status of the Civilian Population by Race, Sex, and Age.* Bureau of Labor Statistics. Retrieved July 20, 2018.

the past—and one we must try to correct," but also said "on the-job train-ing [is] the main route whereby the unskilled have become skilled— [and minimum wage laws have] thus denied them."

Minimum wage laws are not only an attack on the property rights of business owners, but they are also an attack on the property rights of the low-skilled population as a whole. In order for a business to thrive, the owner must be able to do more than sell product or services; he must be able to manage his expenditures in a way that consistently yields a net pos-itive revenue. If a laborer is unable to generate more value than the mini-mum wage dictates the owner must pay him, then the owner will be forced to terminate his employment and pass on his responsibilities to the other workers. Otherwise, the constant yielding of a net negative will ultimately be such a drain on the business as a whole, it will likely mean the closing of the business entirely, thus putting *all* of the employees out of work.

While minimum wage, corporate earnings, and corporate taxes are at the forefront of economic discussion, they are by no means the only parts that make the U.S. economy a crony form of capitalism. Federally, as well as at the state and local levels, barriers to entry erode away the freedom of the market. Texas has a reputation of being a shining exam-ple of a free market economy, and relative to other States, it is, but the keyword is "relative."

Take, for instance, getting your haircut. You tell your cosmetologist or barber what you want and tip them based on their experience, which is typically anticlimactic. You might have even spotted the cosmetology or barber license they have on display at their booth but probably never gave it much thought. That license, however, cost the person who cut your hair anywhere from $5,000 to $20,000, plus the cost of their tools (e.g. scissors, combs, brushes, hair dryers, etc.), textbooks, and other miscellaneous costs. The state of Texas requires by law that a cosmetologist complete 1,500 hours from a licensed cosmetology school, plus pay the state a $50 licens-ing fee. If they wanted to be a licensed barber (which would grant them the ability to use a straight razor to shave their client), it requires an addi-tional 300 hours from a licensed barber school and a $55 licensing fee.[64]

---

64 Texas Occupations Code, Section 1602.254. Retrieved from https://www.tdlr.texas.gov/cosmet/cosmetlaw.htm#1602254.

All of this is required to legally cut hair in Texas. If Texas had a truly free market, then it would not require businesses, schools, or employees to obtain a state license before engaging in their trade. This idea seems to scare people into believing that without the state's involvement ensuring that the schools are teaching proper, safe, and hygienic hair cutting, then the schools' standards would charge tuition to teach people to do little more than butcher people's hair, or that schools would cease to exist entirely, and salons would only hire imbeciles who accidentally slit their customer's throats due to incompetence. These fears are entirely irrational. The free market will dictate the standards that must be applied, and failure to abide by those will negatively affect the business. Yes, it is true that eliminating these licensing and training requirements will allow someone with no formal cosmetology training to cut hair, but that is essentially the point. If they are good at what they do, then they will succeed in that field. If they are not, then they will fail. Cosmetology and barber schools will still exist in such a free market system and still be desirable by salon owners regardless of requirements from the state. Competition in the free market will mandate that salons hire or lease their chairs to the best they can afford, and that will actually increase consumer satisfaction.

This same logic should be applied to every single industry across the board, because there is a capitalistic solution to every economic problem. All that the state's involvement in the free market does is artificially inflate the price of everything by raising the cost of overhead, thereby increasing the cost of the product or service to the end user. It should be understood as a general rule that a business will never truly pay for anything mandated by the state, because that cost will always be rolled over into the price of the final product for the consumer to pay; and fundamentally, there is nothing immoral or wrong with this. As stated earlier, the purpose of a business is to grow and be profitable. It cannot do either if the state adds any barriers or intrusions into its businesses, which ultimately raise their costs on everything it does. Businesses have literally had to spend tens of thousands of dollars on wheelchair ramps, handicapped parking spaces, lowering mirrors in bathrooms by a matter of inches, licensing, inspections, fines, regulatory requirements, and countless other mandates, of which 100% of the financial burden is always passed on to the consumer.

Regulatory costs as a whole are egregiously large across all industries, some of which are more than others. Manufacturing, for example, has a much higher regulatory burden than most other industries. The National Association of Manufactures released a report in 2014 that said the following:

> *"The National Association of Manufacturers (NAM) has issued a new report that shows the macroeconomic impact of federal regulations. The study also reveals the extent to which manufacturers bear a disproportionate share of the regulatory burden, and that burden is heaviest on small manufacturers because their compliance costs are often not affected by economies of scale. The analysis finds that the average U.S. company pays $9,991 per employee per year to comply with federal regulations. The average manufacturer in the United States pays nearly double that amount—$19,564 per employee per year. Small manufacturers, or those with fewer than 50 employees, incur regulatory costs of $34,671 per employee per year. This is more than three times the cost borne by the average U.S. company."*[65]

The report further highlighted that the total compliance costs of federal regulations in manufacturing was $2.028 trillion industry-wide. The cost of compliance for the average U.S. manufacturing firm is $233,182, or about 21% of its average payroll. The bulk of this is not money that is collected by the federal government. It is primarily money that was spent on contractors to bring their facility up to code, money spent on useless state-mandated training programs, and other superfluous things not mandated by the free market. These unnecessary mandates are incredibly burdensome for most in the industry, and the report indicates that "eighty-eight percent of those surveyed say that federal regulations are a top challenge for their firm."[66]

65 National Association of Manufacturers. (2014). "The Cost of Federal Regulation to the U.S. Economy, Manufacturing, and Small Business (Executive Summary)".
66 National Association of Manufacturers. (2014).

These regulatory burdens are not indicative of a free market. There are costs associated with doing business, but none that should be mandated by the state. For liberty to thrive, the market must be free. The freer the market, the freer the people, because the market *is* the people. Regulatory burdens, the minimum wage, business taxation, licensing requirements, minimum standards, and every other state intrusion into the market do nothing but artificially inflate the price of goods and services. Businesses need to operate on their own merit and be driven by nothing other than growing their businesses. Profit motive is a very powerful thing, and that power ultimately lies with the people that make up the market. We have the ultimate say in which businesses thrive and which businesses fail. This is not some utopian idea that will bring happiness and prosperity to everyone. There is no such thing as a guarantee, unlike the socialist model. Some businesses will operate in manners in which you and others may not like, but it might not be a big deal for the majority. In this case, yes, that company will continue to drive profits, but that is okay. You as an individual have the ultimate choice on whether or not to be a customer.

Workers should be given the opportunity to show their value to any prospective employer. As a novice worker learns the tricks of his particular trade, his value will naturally increase as his apprenticeship hones his skills. This will give him the tools necessary to renegotiate his wage with his current employer or seek out higher wages elsewhere. If, however, he is priced out of the market by minimum wage laws, he will never be given the opportunity to learn these skills, depriving him of future property to which he would otherwise be entitled.

Americans have become so reliant on the state that it is hard for many of them to imagine any aspect of life completely free of its involvement, but I challenge everyone to try. Capitalism, unlike socialism, does not promise rainbows and unicorns, does not guarantee success or prevent failure, and will not be free of corruption, but no system will be. There is no solution to the equation of life's guarantees other than death, but the one thing that capitalism can guarantee is that people will have the freedom to choose those with whom they do business based on their merit. Capitalism maximizes the amount of liberty that the individual has, and that is the one thing for which we should always strive.

Before 2009, Uber did not exist, and there were no regulatory burdens for such a company. Within a few years, the company grew at an exponential rate and became a household name. It was at that point that the state began regulating the ride-sharing industry, and their growth began to decline. This is what happens when we let the free market be a free market. Let startups enter without state obstruction and let mega-corporations go bankrupt if they mismanage their finances. Let the little girl sell lemonade on her street corner, and let that taco truck continue to sell great tacos around town. Most importantly, we should let all of this happen freely. It does not take a professor of economics to see that businesses will thrive if we let them. Truly opening up the market will reduce costs, increase competition, and pave the way for exponentially more innovation than we see even today.

Chapter 5

The Greatest Heist in Human History

"The Federal Reserve System is nothing more than legalized counterfeit."
– Ron Paul

I f there is one thing that is sure to trigger roughly 100% of libertarians, as well as a substantial percentage of conservatives, it has to be the Federal Reserve. While most Americans might only know about the Fed solely because every bill in their wallets says "Federal Reserve Note" on it, it is an entity that should be discussed and understood thoroughly. To understand the Fed, it is imperative that we first understand the history of banking, as well as the history of money itself.

The Fed is a subject that is deliberately convoluted, complex, and confusing, and most Americans are blind to what it does. If you crave the restoration of liberty, then it is essential knowledge that must be learned and spread as soon as possible. The Fed is the subject of a lot of conspiracy theories and "forbidden knowledge" themes, but this chapter will stick only to what is definitively provable, and it is tailored for the person who has little-to-no knowledge about the Fed and how it operates.

American currency has its roots in 1775, when the Continental Congress began issuing paper currency known as "Continentals." These notes never took off for several reasons, but the main failure was due to a complete lack of any tangible backing, massive overprinting of notes, and egregious counterfeiting by the British. This devalued the currency so much, that the famous phrase "not worth a Continental" was coined. [67]

Following the Revolutionary War, the idea of a central bank was hotly debated between Thomas Jefferson and Alexander Hamilton, but it was much more complex than just creating a bank. The entire purpose of

---

67 Newman, Eric P. (1990). *"The Early Paper Money of America."*

a central bank is to serve as a medium of credit to the nation, and serve as the holder of the public debt, which Hamilton viewed as essential to securing the nation's finances. As Treasury Secretary, Hamilton wrote the following to the House of Representatives in January of 1790 concerning the then $71 million national debt:[68]

> *"And as on the one hand, the necessity for borrowing in particular emergencies cannot be doubted, so on the other, it is equally evident, that to be able to borrow upon good terms, it is essential that the credit of a nation should be well established. For when the credit of a country is in any degree questionable, it never fails to give an extravagant premium, in one shape or another, upon all the loans it has occasion to make. Nor does the evil end here; the same disadvantage must be sustained upon whatever is to be bought on terms of future payment... With regard to the instalments of the foreign debt, these, in the opinion of the Secretary, ought to be paid by new loans abroad."[69]*

Hamilton's view was that the public debt, if not excessive, was a blessing to the nation, as it would establish good credit for any willing lenders at a future date. Conversely, Jefferson despised both the ideas of a central bank and of perpetual debt. The animosity between the two men was so significant that other historical figures of the time have had their ideologies described as Jeffersonian or Hamiltonian. The feud was bitter indeed, and the notion that these two men detested each other would be a severe understatement. In an impassioned letter to President Washington dated September 9, 1792, Jefferson laid out the quintessential difference between himself and Hamilton, all while defending himself against a political hit piece by his nemesis:

> *"[M]y objection to the constitution was that it wanted a bill of rights securing freedom of religion, freedom of the press, freedom from stand-*

---

68 "Historical Debt Outstanding – Annual 1790–1849." Retrieved from https://www.treasurydirect.gov/govt/reports/pd/histdebt/histdebt_histo1.htm.

69 *The Papers of Alexander Hamilton*, Vol. 6, Edited by Harold C. Syrett. (1962). Retrieved from http://www.wwnorton.com/college/history/archive/resources/documents/ch08_02.htm.

ing armies, trial by jury, & a constant Habeas corpus act. Colo Hamilton's was that it wanted a king and a house of lords. The sense of America has approved my objection & added a bill of rights, not the king and lords... The second charge is equally untrue. My whole correspondence while in France, & every word, letter, & act on the subject since my return, prove that no man is more ardently intent to see the public debt soon & sacredly paid off than I am. This exactly marks the difference between Colo Hamilton's views & mine, that I would wish the debt paid to morrow; he wishes it never to be paid, but always to be a thing to corrupt & manage the legislature."[70]

By this time, however, America's first central bank, the Bank of the United States (BUS) was already established. Hamilton had successfully convinced Congress and President Washington of the BUS's necessity, and it was chartered for a term of twenty years on February 25, 1791 (though it did not open until December 12 of that year). The BUS not only served as the holder of the public debt, but also as a commercial bank. Here, individuals and businesses could open accounts and take out loans, just like we can at our banks of choice today.

In 1792, Congress passed the first Coinage Act, which established and defined the U.S. Dollar as the base unit of money. The Act placed the dollar on a bimetal standard of gold and silver and created various units of money from $10 gold eagles (containing 16 grams of pure gold) to half dimes (containing 1.2 grams of pure silver). Cents and half-cents (containing 17 grams and 8.5 grams respectively of pure copper) were also defined, but as the Act's title said, everything was coinage.[71]

From the collapse of the Continental currency during the Revolution, all the way until after the Civil War, the United States did not have a standard paper currency. Banks throughout the several states would issue banknotes in lieu of gold and silver coin when loans were issued. This way, they could keep real money in reserve should someone come along wishing to make a withdrawal. The banknotes were effectively the

---

70 Jefferson, Thomas. (September 9, 1792). "The Conflict with Hamilton. To the President of the United States." *Writings.*
71 Coinage Act of 1792. 1 Stat. 246. Retrieved from https://web.archive.org/web/20040407164627/http://nesara.org/files/coinage_act_1792.pdf.

same as paper currency today, but they each bore the name of the bank of issue on its face and the bank's own design. This resulted in confusion and frustration throughout the nation. Notes issued by Bank A would be accepted by Bank B, but at a discount to cover the costs associated with transferring the notes back to Bank A in exchange for gold. As an example, if you had a $20 note from New York State Bank but found yourself in Georgia, the Georgia State Bank would accept the note but not at the full face value (e.g. $15). Thus that $20 note was worth less than $20 outside of New York.

The federal government had 20% ownership of the BUS itself, and the remaining 80% was owned by private investors (though all of them were minority shareholders). Regardless, the federal government garnered profits from the BUS, and because of its hand in banking, many feared it could turn into a monopolistic powerhouse that could be detrimental to the economy. The BUS had eight branches, and though it was prohibited from purchasing government bonds, notes from the BUS were the only notes acceptable to pay federal taxes (which were primarily from import duties at the time).

Unease grew when the power the BUS wielded came to light. Though it was never officially charged with the power of setting monetary policy, or even controlling state banks, their power and connection to the federal government allowed them to do that very thing. In order to attempt to control inflation and deflation, the BUS would hold state banknotes in their vaults for a period and subsequently dump them back to the issuing bank for reclamation of gold. This allowed the BUS to control the number of notes in issuance, thus controlling the value of the dollar.[72] What exactly was the problem though? Should the interests of the nation not want to control inflation? Throughout history, every attempt to control the will of the free market, both maliciously and benevolently, has been met with long term negative consequences. What made these attempts unique was that it was done by an entity that was 80% owned by private investors, and their de facto control over every bank in the country definitely warranted concern.

---

72 Hill, Andrew T. (December 4, 2015). "The First Bank of the United States." *Federal Reserve History.*

During the two decades of the BUS's existence, both bankers and the people grew weary of the BUS's power to control currency, and this made it customary at the time to deal in Spanish and French specie (gold and silver coin). Hamilton had drafted plans to prohibit the use of foreign coin that were supposed to take effect as soon as 1795, but their popularity caused these plans to be postponed for over 60 years.[73]

At the time the BUS's charter expired in 1811, the buying power of the American dollar had dropped by 28% and would not regain its value until after the War of 1812 ended. This was in spite of a Second BUS's creation in 1816, which operated under a very similar scope to its predecessor. It was created out of a panic due to the further devaluation of the dollar caused by war, which can be seen in the chart on page 89 (which I recommend using in tandem with reading the rest of this chapter).

Throughout the twenty years of the Second BUS, the confidence and buying power of the dollar showed amazing growth, and in 1828, the dollar was actually 1% more valuable than its 1792 counterpart, but a different problem surfaced; it did not stop climbing. In 1833, the dollar was worth nearly 14% more than the 1792 dollar, and both markets and governments fear deflation almost as much as they fear inflation. Think of inflation and deflation as similar to trading stocks but in reverse.

Basic stock trading strategy is to buy low and sell high, but in the case of the buying power of the dollar, "buying" is obtaining debt, and "selling" is paying it off. If you take out a loan for $10,000 when the dollar is worth only 80¢ with payments deferred for one year, and the following year, the dollar is worth $1.20, the belief is that the real value of your debt has grown by an additional 50%, and though the principle of the loan will still be $10,000, it will be as if you had actually taken out a loan for $15,000. In such a case, because the dollar has become stronger, wages begin to decrease, and stock prices begin to drop. People tend to view this negatively, even though it can just be the market correcting itself (which ultimately stabilizes its value). In a perfect world, $1 would always be worth $1, not 80¢ nor $1.20. The world, unfortunately, is not perfect despite state's attempts to make it so.

---

73 Muhl, Gerard. (2001). "When Foreign Coins Circulated Freely". *The Crooked Lake Review*.

In 1834, Congress decided to act in order to curb the growth of the dollar's value, and reduced the ratio of gold in Eagles from 15:1 to 16:1. This had the effect Congress was seeking, and the dollar devalued steadily until 1837, where it was worth exactly the same as the 1792 dollar. The year prior, the Second BUS's charter expired and was not renewed, and the nearly three-decade-long era known as the "free banking era" began.

From 1836 until 1863, all banks in the U.S. were state-chartered banks, and in the case of Michigan, banks did not need to be chartered by the legislature if they met the minimum requirements set by law. The number of banks throughout the U.S. boomed, and reports of thievery, swindling, and conning by bankers began to increase as well. The era was dubbed by historians as "wildcat banking," and most writing on the subject highlights the victims of con artists due to lack of state oversight and the state's failure to address the issue of banks purchasing notes of competitors at a discounted rate. Like most things throughout history, however, the volume of these accounts seems to be exaggerated. Former Federal Reserve Chairman Alan Greenspan (1987-2006) said the following on the subject:

> *"While free banking was not actually as free as commonly perceived, it also was not nearly as unstable. The perception of the free banking era as an era of 'wildcat' banking marked by financial instability and, in particular, by widespread significant losses to noteholders also turns out to be exaggerated. Recent scholarship has demonstrated that free bank failures were not as common, and resulting losses to noteholders were not as severe as earlier historians had claimed... Between 1838 and 1860 the discounts on notes of new entrants diminished and discounts came to correspond more closely to objective measures of the riskiness of individual banks.*
>
> *Part of this reduction in riskiness was a reflection of improvement in state regulation and supervision. Part was also private market regulation in an environment in which depositor and note holders were not protected by a safety net. That is, the moral hazard we all spend so much time worrying about today had not yet been introduced into the system."*[74]

---

74 Greenspan, Alan. (May 2, 1998). "Our Banking History." *The Federal Reserve Board.* Retrieved from https://www.federalreserve.gov/boarddocs/speeches/1998/19980502.htm.

Evaluation of the consumer price index indicates that during the free banking era, the value of the dollar peaked in 1843 at 130% of the 1792 dollar (primarily due to the end of the Panic of 1837), and bottomed out at 95% in 1862 due to the Civil War.[75] All things considered, the era of free banking averaged a 16% stronger dollar compared to 16% weaker dollar throughout the 44 years (and two BUS's) that took place prior. Had the state just left the dollar alone, its value would have been corrected by the market, and it would have stabilized over the long term.

The Civil War took a detrimental toll on the value of the dollar. At the war's onset in 1861, the dollar was worth about $1.09, and by the end of the war in 1865, it was worth only 59¢. The chaos stemmed from the splitting of the nation, and since all banking at the outbreak of the war was done by state-chartered banks, banknotes from southern banks became worthless in the North, and vice versa. In 1863, Congress again took it upon themselves to try and fix the issue and passed a series of acts known as the National Bank Acts. These acts did not establish another central bank like the BUS, but did establish a national currency, regulated banking very strictly, allowed for banks to be chartered by Congress, and taxed state-chartered banks significantly. The tax was so cumbersome on state-chartered banks that by the war's end, most of them had either collapsed entirely or received charters from Congress.[76]

The value of the dollar slowly recovered after the war, taking until 1885 to get back to 99% of its original 1792 value. State banks also slowly began making a comeback into existence, and the mandate set by the National Bank Acts requiring the face value exchange of national notes helped the dollar recover. One aspect that delayed recovery was the issuance of fiat currency that was not redeemable for gold (known as greenbacks) to help pay for war efforts, though in 1873, Congress ended the bimetal standard and put the U.S. dollar firmly on the gold standard. The dollar continued its rise until 1897, when it settled at 116% of its 1792 value, and then slowly began creeping back down until 1914 with

75 Based on an analysis of Consumer Price Index data compiled from https://www.officialdata.org/.
76 Dieterle, David A.; Simmons, Katherine M. (2014). *Government and the Economy: An Encyclopedia.*

the establishment of the Federal Reserve System and the outbreak of World War I.

War is hell. Aside from the fact that almost every war in which the U.S. has been involved since the 1950s has had nothing to do with defending our national sovereignty, it is also incredibly expensive. The massive expense associated with war causes the buying power of the dollar to drop substantially. Throughout history, kingdoms, empires, and even the United States took on massive debt to pay for every war in which they have been involved. In the times where money reigned, gold was borrowed, and gold was paid back with interest. When currency was invented to serve as a representation of money, however, the dawn of perpetual debt became inevitable.

Bankers only had so much gold in their vaults, but they had an endless supply of paper. Throughout the eras of banking prior to the Federal Reserve's implementation, bankers would at least be compelled to minimize how many excess notes they printed. Too many non-backed notes would have detrimental consequences to the bank itself at the very least. In today's post-monetary era, those laws need not apply, and thus brings us to the creation of the Federal Reserve System.

In October of 1907, a 50% plunge of the New York Stock Exchange's peak from the previous year led to an infamous banking crisis known as the Panic of 1907. Fritz Augustus Heinze was one of three major copper tycoons in the United States (known as the "Copper Kings"), and was the founder of the United Copper Company. He also was heavily involved in banking with his good friend Charles W. Morse, "with whom he served on at least six national banks, ten state banks, five trust companies, and four insurance companies."[77]

Heinze, his brother, Otto, and Morse schemed to manipulate the stock price of United Copper in order to corner the entire copper market. When the plan failed, the price of United Copper's stock plummeted from $60 per share to $10 in just two days.[78] To put this into perspective,

77 Spellen, Suzanne. (January 16, 2014). "Walkabout: Charles W. Morse: King of New York". *Brownstoner*.
78 Arandia, Mathilde. (August 13, 2010). "The Fame and Folly of Cornering a Market". *Fortune*.

in August of 2000, the stock price of Enron was fluctuating around $90 per share, at which point investors began to lose confidence in the company, and the stock price began to steadily drop. By November of 2001, the company's now infamous scandal became publicly known, their stock price, then at just around $10 per share, plummeted to just $0.26 per share. This was a loss of 99% of the company's stock valuation over the course of 15 months.[79] United Copper, conversely, lost over 83% practically overnight.

Following the plunge of United Copper's stock price, depositors with accounts held by Mercantile National Bank (of which Heinze was president) began rushing to withdraw their deposits (an act known as "bank runs"). Despite the fact that Mercantile National was still solvent, depositors believed Heinze and his ventures to be bankrupt after the scandal, and in their panic, it became a self-fulfilling prophecy. To make matters worse, it was also revealed that Charles T. Barney (president of one of the largest banks in the U.S., Knickerbocker Trust Company) was also heavily involved in the scheme, and depositors began running on it as well. In one day, depositors had withdrawn nearly $8 million (over $221.5 million today) from Knickerbocker Trust, and the bank was forced to suspend all operations.[80]

In the years that followed, history says that the nation's leading bankers sought to prevent, or at least control, the types of events that led to the Panic of 1907. To do this, control was not *really* needed over the banks themselves, but over the currency instead. Essentially, the mentality was that if the state could put people's minds at ease that their "money" would always be there, even if their bank disappeared overnight, then bank runs would become a thing of the past. With that kind of control over the nation's currency, the banks would be controlled by default. This brings us to a Republican Senator from the state of Rhode Island, Nelson W. Aldrich.

First appointed to the U.S. Senate by the Rhode Island General Assembly in 1881, by the turn of the century, Senator Aldrich had become incredibly powerful in the Congress' upper chamber as the Senate Finance Committee Chairman. In 1908, he cosponsored the Aldrich-Vreeland Act which established the National Monetary Commission, which Aldrich

---

79 Benston, George J. (November 6, 2003). "The Quality of Corporate Financial Statements and their Auditors Before and After Enron".
80 Moen, Jon R. and Tallman, Ellis W. (December 4, 2015). "The Panic of 1907". *Federal Reserve History*.

himself headed.[81] The Commission's purpose was to study the reasons behind the Panic of 1907, as well as the banking and monetary laws of the United States, and those of European nations, and ultimately craft a solution to prevent another financial crisis.

In 1909, Aldrich cosponsored the Payne-Aldrich Tariff Act, which ultimately split Republicans between progressives and conservatives within the Party. The Act passed in April, and was signed by President Taft, but the infighting continued. To try and lull the debates, Aldrich authored what became the 16th Amendment in July, despite previously calling income tax "communistic."[82] Supposedly, Senator Aldrich and other Congressional conservatives actually opposed the implementation of income tax, but they thought that the proposed amendment would temporarily appease the progressive Republican's calls for higher tariffs, and it would never get ratified by three-fourths of the state legislatures. Despite this attempt to defuse the infighting, Republicans lost control of the House following the 1910 midterms.

Less than two weeks after the midterm elections, under the guise of attending a "duck hunt," Senator Aldrich and his personal secretary, Arthur Shelton, secretly met with Assistant Secretary of the U.S. Treasury Dr. A. Piatt Andrew, J.P. Morgan & Co. senior partner Henry P. Davison, National City Bank president Frank A. Vanderlip, Kuhn, Loeb, & Co. partner Paul M. Warburg, and Benjamin Strong, Jr. (who represented J.P. Morgan himself). The meeting lasted for ten days, and by the end of it, the men crafted the foundation of what would become the Federal Reserve System.[83]

Four months later, Senator Aldrich retired from the Senate. He remained chairman of the National Monetary Commission until it issued its final report to Congress on January 8, 1912. By this time, 31 of the required 36 states had ratified the income tax amendment, and three more would do so that year: Arizona, Minnesota, and Louisiana. The Senate had filed a bill with Aldrich's plan from the Commission's final report, but it went nowhere that session.

---

81 *"Aldrich-Vreeland Act"*. (1908). 35 Stat. 546. Retrieved from http://legisworks.org/sal/35/stats/STATUTE-35-Pg546.pdf
82 Sternstein, Jerome L. (1974). "Encyclopedia of American Biography".
83 Bagwell, Tyler E. "The Jekyll Island Duck Hunt that Created the Federal Reserve". Retrieved from http://www.jekyllislandhistory.com/federalreserve.shtml

In June, ahead of the 1912 Presidential Election, the Democratic Party adopted a platform plank opposing "the so-called Aldrich bill or the establishment of a central bank." The continued infighting between progressive and conservative Republicans resulted in Democrats retaking control of both the Senate and the White House.[84] A month following Delaware's ratification of the 16th Amendment (making it officially a part of the constitution, and thus authorizing the federal government to institute an income tax), the 63rd Congress began on March 4, 1913. On June 23rd, President Woodrow Wilson addressed a joint session of Congress, and a baffling paradigm shift between the two major political parties happened seemingly instantaneously.

"It is absolutely imperative that we should give the business men of this country a banking and currency system by means of which they can make use of the freedom of enterprise and of individual initiative which we are about to bestow upon them...

"The tyrannies of business, big and little, lie within the field of credit. We know that. Shall we not act upon the knowledge? Do we not know how to act upon it? If a man cannot make his assets available at pleasure, his assets of capacity and character and resource, what satisfaction is it to him to see opportunity beckoning to him on every hand, when others have the keys of credit in their pockets and treat them as all but their own private possession? It is perfectly clear that it is our duty to supply the new banking and currency system the country needs, and it will need it immediately more than it has ever needed it before."[85]

Because a Democratic president called for the establishment of a central bank, Democrats now supported it and Republicans now opposed it. Two days following the President's speech to Congress, Democratic Congressman Carter Glass of Virginia introduced H.R. 7837 in the House with the short title, "The Federal Reserve Act." There were differences

---

84 Democratic Party Platform, 1912 (June 25, 1912). Retrieved from https://www.presidency.ucsb.edu/documents/1912-democratic-party-platform
85 Wilson, Woodrow. (June 23, 1913). Retrieved from https://www.llsdc.org/assets/FRAdocs/fra-lh_v50-cr-2132-2133_wilson.pdf

between Congressman Glass' bill and the Aldrich plan, but most of them were semantical in nature (such as the length of the charter, the number of members on the board, who appoints those members, etc.).

A few months went by as the bill went through its cycle of proceedings, and in September, it came to the floor of the House. After presenting an in-depth comparison of the Glass and Aldrich plans, Republican Congressman Simeon Fess of Ohio said the following:

> *"What does this comparison show? The bill before us is in many features a copy of the Aldrich plan. The chief difference is in the control of the system... [The Aldrich plan] invested operation in the banker's power without permitting sufficient regulation by the public. This gave undue influence and power to the money classes, which may be serious. What does the Glass bill do? ...It virtually takes the banking business out of the hands of the owners and places it in the grasp of the Government. To be specific, it makes the Government the operative agent, the administrative factor, instead of limiting it to the regulatory or controlling function.*
>
> *"As the Aldrich bill gave too much power to the banks, the Glass bill gives too much power to the Government, or too little power to the owners of the property being administered."*

The Federal Reserve Act passed the House two days later on September 18 with a vote of 287-85. The vote was largely down the newly-established party lines with only 3 Democrats and 81 Republicans voting *nay*. Surprisingly, one of the 31 Republican *yea* votes came from the aforementioned Congressman Fess, who also made these prophetic comments in his speech:

> *"This bill attempts to renew the dangerous dogma that the Government can make money value by its decree. 'Fiat' has taken such a deep hold upon a portion of our people that it springs up at every passing chance... We probably will never be free of that class of thinkers which... clamored for more Continental money 'not worth a continental;' that believed a confederacy could by simple decree give purchasing power to a currency stamped by the Confederate Government; that assured the world that*

even in time of storm and stress of civil war, ...all that was needed to prosecute such a war was for the Government to use its prerogative, place its stamp upon a piece of paper, thereby decreeing it money, and it would be money and perform all the functions of money need. In other words, we are assured that the fiat of the Government is the essential thing. This financial school of coin denies the intrinsic value of a standard, ignores the need for specie, and pins its faith upon Government decree...

"There are two very significant items in this provision for note issue that demand careful scrutiny – the redemption feature and the legal-tender feature. The notes are to be redeemed in gold or lawful money on demand. This pretends to preserve the gold standard, but in reality, it may mean its abandonment..."[86]

Oklahoma Senator Robert Owen sponsored the bill in the Senate, and after a few tweaks and corroborations with the House, the final bill passed on December 23, 1913 with a vote of 43-25 (again down party lines with all 25 *nay* votes coming from the 28 voting Republicans). That same evening, President Wilson added his signature establishing the Federal Reserve System in the United States. The *New York Times* front page blazed the headline *"President's Signature Enacts Currency Law."* One could speculate that the use of the euphemism "currency law" was due to the Democratic Party platform plank against establishing a central bank.

Throughout the decades since 1913, the Federal Reserve Act has been amended a number of times, almost always to grant the Fed more power over the various banks across the country. In 1927, the twenty-year charter of the Fed was extended indefinitely, which is arguably the worst amendment ever made.

Fully explaining how the Fed "works" is not an easy task, and some would argue that it is not even possible. The entire Federal Reserve System is so convoluted and complex, that despite the literal volumes upon volumes of writings on the subject, it is unlikely that anyone can really know all of the inner workings. This will be merely a very basic Campbell's soup version.

---

86 Fess, S. D. (September 16, 1913). "Speech of Hon. S. D. Fess, of Ohio, in the House of Representatives". Retrieved from https://www.llsdc.org/assets/FRAdocs/fra-1h_v50-cr-a282-a289.pdf

Remember how Congressman Fess proclaimed that the Glass bill gave too much power to the federal government? The problem with that statement is the fact that the Federal Reserve is a *private* bank that is not a part of any branch of the federal government. It has a .gov website, a fancy flag, a great seal, and all seven members of the Board of Governors are nominated by the President of the United States (and confirmed by the Senate for a 14-year term), but it is not a government entity in any official capacity. Fess was right in that the federal government has control of the System through the Board, but the fact remains that the System itself is not tied to the government.

The hierarchy of the Federal Reserve System is convoluted, but this is essentially the various roles that have been set up:[87]

- The Board of Governors (7 members)
  - All 7 are nominated by the President and confirmed by the Senate
- The Federal Reserve Banks (12 Banks)
  - Each Fed Bank controls its specific district
  - Most Fed Banks have Fed Branches (24 in total)
  - Each Fed Bank has a 9-member Board of Directors (3 classes of 3 members)
    - Class A – Elected by Member Banks in the district to represent those banks
    - Class B – Elected by Member Banks to represent the public (presumably by magic)
    - Class C – Appointed by the Board of Governors
  - Fed Bank President is nominated by a committee of Class B and Class C Directors and confirmed by the Board of Governors
- Member Bank
  - A private bank that is a member of its district's Fed Bank by receiving a charter from the U.S. Treasury
  - Chances are, your bank of choice is a Member Bank

---

87 "Roles and Responsibilities of Federal Reserve Directors". *Federal Reserve System Publication.* Retrieved from https://www.federalreserve.gov/aboutthefed/directors/pdf/roles_responsibilities_FINALweb013013.pdf

Technically speaking, the member banks are the actual "owners" of the Federal Reserve, but they have very little power. The Federal Open Market Committee (FOMC) is where the real power lies. This is a committee consisting of all seven members of the Board and five of the twelve Bank presidents. They are required by law to meet four times per year but typically meet at least eight times, and the meeting is always behind closed doors. Usually, the biggest news coming from this meeting is what the Fed is going to do with its interest rate (the rate at which it loans "money" to member banks).

This interest rate can have a huge impact on the economy as a whole. When you apply for a loan, it is the Fed's interest rate that ultimately dictates your interest rate, regardless of what lender you choose. If the Fed alters its interest rate by even 0.25% during a time of economic uncertainty, the entire economy can enter a recession or depression. The power that the Fed wields with this interest rate is amazing, but it is nothing compared to its power to fabricate currency.

Every note printed by the U.S. Treasury says "Federal Reserve Note" on it because the Treasury does not control the printing of currency; the Fed does. The Treasury regularly sells bonds to anyone willing to buy them. Bonds are nothing more than a promissory note for a loan from the buyer, which gets repaid with interest after it matures. When the Fed wants to increase the currency supply, it takes custody of x number of Treasury bonds, and the Treasury prints that amount in currency. That currency is then sent to the Fed Banks to hold for loans to its member banks. This increases the supply of the currency in circulation, and devalues the dollar. After those bonds mature, the Treasury has to pay the Fed the value of those bonds, plus interest.[88] The Fed never actually paid for those bonds, however. It merely took custody of them. This means that not only is the Fed the holder the national debt, it *owns* the national debt via a complex money laundering scheme.

Think of it like this: Robert has possession of the only dollar in existence, and you need it. Robert offers to loan you the dollar, but on the condition that you have to pay him back $2 after one year. If it is the

---

88 Petroff, Eric. (October 5, 2018). "The Fed's Tools for Influencing the Economy". *Investopedia.*

only dollar in existence, how do you pay back $2? Simple. Robert creates $2 to loan to you on the condition that you pay him back $4 on that loan. So now you have possession of $3, but you owe $6. No matter what, you will never be able to pay back anything other than the principle of the loan, because that is all that exists. The relationship between the Fed and the Treasury is the same, with the caveat that the Fed does not actually possess any dollars; it just tells the Treasury when they can print more.

Another major power the Fed, and subsequently, its member banks, has is a process known as fractional reserve banking. This is another means by which the banks themselves create "money" out of thin air. The Fed establishes reserve requirements for its member banks, which is a mandate for the amount of cash the bank is required to keep on hand as a percentage of its deposits. This is currently set by the Fed at 10% for banks with transaction accounts of more than $124.2 million, which means that should a bank have $250 million in transaction accounts, they are required to keep $25 million in cash.[89] The rest is loaned out to customers. The scheme works like this with the 10% figure:

- You have a $100 bill and deposit it into a new bank account.
- The bank takes your $100 and loans John $90 from your account (replacing the $90 in your account with IOUs).
- Your balance still shows $100, but John now has $90 in cash, and buys a widget from Robert for that price.
- Robert deposits that $90 into his bank, and they loan Stacy $81 from his account (again, replacing the $81 in his account with IOUs).
- The process repeats… and repeats… and repeats.
- Magically, your initial $100 deposit has "created" an additional $1,000 of IOUs that did not exist.

The creation of this digital currency is based on a reserve factor of 10%, but that is just the requirements for some banks. The other reserve requirements set by the Fed are 3%, and even 0% depending upon the

---

89 Retrieved from https://www.federalreserve.gov/monetarypolicy/reservereq.htm on June 2, 2019.

amount of transactional accounts. This means that smaller banks with less than $17 million in transaction accounts as of this writing do not have to keep *anything* in reserve and can loan out 100% of your account balance without your knowledge or consent. The Fed can also change these requirements at will. During the 2020 COVID-19 pandemic, the Fed removed *all* reserve requirements for all banks regardless of their transaction accounts, allowing them to lend out 100% of the cash they had on hand.[90] Quite literally every dollar currently in circulation is just a representation of debt, both the state's and yours.

As stated in Chapter 3, the interest paid in 2020 was $478.8 billion, or about 13.1% of the total revenue taken in by the federal government, and it is only expected to grow. By 2028, the Congressional Budget Office projects that annual interest on the debt will be $915 billion, which is more than 2018's entire Department of Defense budget.[91] The more debt the Fed owns, the more the dollar decreases in value.

Prior to the Federal Reserve, the most devaluation the U.S. dollar ever faced was in 1814 when the War of 1812 devalued the dollar by 54.64% of its original value (which steadily bounced back over a decade). Today, because of the Federal Reserve's existence, the dollar has lost 96.28% of its 1792 value and shows exactly zero signs of any sort of recovery. What $100 can purchase in 2020, could be bought for $3.72 in 1792 (or $3.84 in 1913). Because this devaluation is caused by an entity's direct interference and control, this is unequivocally theft.

Referring back to the chart on page 89, you can see there are two things in particular that have caused a very unstable dollar. The first and most impactful, is war. Every time the United States has been engaged in war, the dollar loses a substantial amount of value. This was at first caused by market uncertainty. Thinking back to the devaluation from the War of 1812, a brand-new nation with a brand-new currency being at war with the economic and military powerhouse of the time would certainly make anyone holding those notes worry about what the future would hold. The

90 Federal Reserve Actions to Support the Flow of Credit to Households and Businesses. (March 15, 2020). Retrieved from https://www.federalreserve.gov/newsevents/pressreleases/monetary20200315b.htm on October 23, 2020.
91 Schwartz, Nelson D. (September 25, 2018). "As Debt Rises, the Government will Soon Spend More on Interest Than on the Military". *The New York Times*.

same would happen if that nation went to war with itself (as we did in 1861). Since taking the title of the world's economic and military leader, the U.S.'s substantial loss in currency value from wars has simply been caused by the amount of debt incurred from the conflicts. To be clear, this was also a big factor with early American currency, but in today's global mind, the worry about the U.S. ceasing to exist no longer factors into that equation.

The second thing that can also be seen from the chart is the state attempting to control the value of the currency. This always seems to make matters worse over the long run, and the reason is because no entity can force a free market solution to happen. Fluctuations in value will always happen regardless of what controls are instituted. The absolute worst thing the federal government did was create the Federal Reserve System, because it has robbed the American people of over 96% of their property's value. Each and every year, the news will report on the annual "inflation" level, but this is a lie. What the Fed is doing to the dollar is not inflation; it is devaluation, and there is a huge difference.

Most of what happened with the dollar during the Free Banking Era was inflation and deflation. The various market aspects had effects on the dollar that would make it adjust accordingly and usually not by much (from a relative standpoint to today). When Congress reduced the silver ratio in small denomination coins in 1853, devaluation of the dollar resulted.

When the Fed came into existence, they were given a total monopoly on U.S. currency. Fueled by an endless revenue stream from income tax, the only thing that initially kept the Fed in check was the gold standard. They could play with and control the amount notes being printed, but they knew that doing it too much would have severe negative consequences (just as private banks did before the national currency was established). The wars against communism increased the national debt substantially, and the gold standard was essentially backing the federal government into a corner. The dollar's value was continuing to drop following the end of World War II, and engagements in Korea just a few years later were not helping matters. The choice was either to find a way to get more "money" to fund war efforts or pull out.

In 1971, President Nixon found the "solution" to the money problem: eliminate it. In what was dubbed the "Nixon shock," President Nixon ordered the Treasury to no longer back the dollar by gold or any asset. This was detrimental to the dollar and is the catalyst behind why the Fed's policies have continued to drive the dollar's value down ever since. Despite Nixon "lay[ing] to rest the bugaboo that is called devaluation," it is clear from the chart that his single action was the final nail in the coffin for the U.S. dollar.[92]

The dollar is broken beyond repair. It is a ruptured fire main of problems that cannot be turned off without severe economic consequences. The $27.8 trillion debt is based off the devalued dollar, so any solution that could be proposed to fix it *must* eliminate the debt entirely first. I made the analogy earlier about taking out a $10,000 loan when the dollar was worth 80¢, and then having the dollar's value rise to $1.20. The dollar amount of the debt remains the same despite the fact that the debt holder's repayment will seem as if it was increased by an additional 50%. If today's dollar was somehow able to regain all of its lost value overnight, the national debt would seem to have grown by over 2,613%! The face value of the debt would still be $27.8 trillion, but the increased value of each dollar would make it seem like paying off a debt of $754.3 trillion.

Where banking has always gone wrong is their ability to issue out notes in excess of their total accounts and only keep a small amount in reserve. This is legalized counterfeit regardless whether the Federal Reserve does it or if a bank does it with fractional reserve banking. Even during the free banking era, both BUS's, or any other point in history, the second a banknote was issued that was not backed by anything held by the issuing bank, counterfeit had taken place. The sole reason that our dollar is as worthless as it is today is entirely due to the Fed's ability to order the Treasury to print notes at their beck and call. The income tax perpetuates this habit, and has locked us into financial slavery. The entire Federal Reserve System has not only robbed us of nearly all of the value of our property but it has enslaved us and future generations to perpetual debt. That is why the Federal Reserve System is the greatest heist in human history.

---

92 Nixon, Richard. (August 15, 1971). "Address to the Nation Outlining a New Economic Policy: 'The Challenge of Peace'." *The American Presidency Project*.

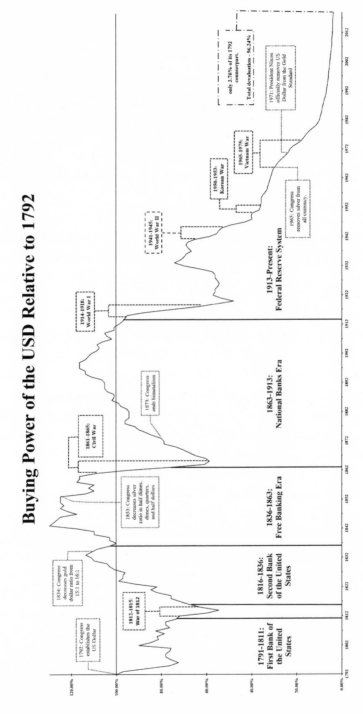

Buying Power of the USD Relative to 1792

Chapter 6

The Privilege of Life

"The right to life does not depend, and must not be declared to be contingent, on the pleasure of anyone else." – Mother Teresa

The right to life is the first inalienable right listed in the Declaration of Independence, as well as every single other work on the topic of natural rights. Life is the single most fundamental natural right there is, for without it, there can be no others. It is also, for some reason, one that has fueled bitter debates on more than one political topic in the U.S.

The Democratic Party cites the right to life as a response to a tragic shooting to push more gun control legislation, or as a justification for universal healthcare. The Republican Party cites it when pushing to ban abortion or for creating more security at the southern border. The Libertarian Party cites it as the reason they oppose capital punishment, but it is never mentioned when they speak of "a woman's right to choose." It, therefore, begs the question as to who is correct when it comes to the right to life. The answer: no one.

The funny thing about life is that it really is a binary topic. Either someone is alive or they are not, and someone who is alive either has the right to remain so, or they do not. If there is any point at which one's philosophy acknowledges the right to life in one area but ignores it in another, then the philosophy is fatally flawed, and they cannot say they support the natural right to life without being hypocritical. First, start with the basic question: is life a natural right? A silly question to be sure, but one that seems to constantly be forgotten when topics shift from one to another.

Let us begin with a simple example. Bob is sitting at a bus stop when Jack decides to shoot and kill him. Is life a natural right? It is hard to imagine anyone answering no in this scenario, so we must change a few variables in order to make it slightly more complex. Bob is a Jew, the year is 1941, and he is sitting at a bus stop in Germany. Jack is a Nazi and follows all laws, regulations, and protocols to take Bob against his will where he is executed. In this scenario, Bob's death was a legal execution sanctioned by the state. Now, the question can be asked a bit more specifically: is life a natural right?

Even with these changes, we would be hard-pressed to find someone to disagree. I highlighted life being taken in this way to illustrate that natural rights still exist, even when the state refuses to acknowledge them as such. This also emphasizes that since natural rights were not granted by society (i.e. the state), they therefore cannot be taken away by society. If the state bore the authority to strip an individual of any natural right, then natural rights do not exist at all. If natural rights do not exist, then there are only privileges contingent upon certain criteria as defined by the state. This should be the end of the discussion, but since there are hotly debated issues surrounding the right to life across various topics, we must do our best to explore these in full.

In the latter scenario, Bob was not guilty of any crime of aggression against anyone else, yet was executed by his government. When the variable of an atrocious criminal act is introduced into the equation, many people begin to change their tune about the right to life. I, myself, used to be a staunch supporter of capital punishment. After all, people on death row have been convicted of very heinous acts against other human beings. For example, on Christmas Eve, 1987, James Eugene Bigby murdered four people over the course of seven hours across Fort Worth and Arlington, TX. One of his victims was a 17-week-old infant named Jayson Kehler, whom he suffocated "with a piece of cellophane, and then placed the child face down in a water-filled sink." Bigby was executed by lethal injection on March 14, 2017.[93] The question, however, remains just as valid: is life a natural right?

James Bigby was guilty of an act so disgusting that the English language does not possess the vocabulary to adequately describe it. This triggers our emotional centers so vehemently that the impulse to con-

---

93 *Texas Department of Criminal Justice*. Executed Offenders – James Eugene Bigby. Retrieved from https://www.tdcj.texas.gov/death_row/dr_info/bigbyjames.jpg

clude that he is not fit to breathe the same air as us is almost too easy to shout from the rooftops. Those who support the death penalty, my past-self included, have often laid the claim that the person "gave up their right to live" when they committed murder. To this, the question must be raised as to whether it is possible to "give up" a natural right. The answer must be no.

Imagine that Bob willingly sells his Ferrari to John. While this voluntary exchange transfers title of ownership over this specific Ferrari from Bob to John, Bob still has the right to own that specific Ferrari again, provided the buyer voluntarily sells it back to him. This is because Bob's natural right to own property generally is unchanged. Is there any circumstance where Bob can give up his right to own that Ferrari or the ownership of property generally? The answer again must be no, as that is what distinguishes a right from a privilege. The same logic applies to the natural right to life. Both life and the right to life are still two different things. If Bob willingly jumps in front of a bus and dies (regardless if he did so solely to kill himself, or if he was trying to save someone else), he still retained his *right* to live, but his voluntary action to jump in front of the bus resulted in him losing his life.

In both scenarios, Bob never gives up his *right* to own property, nor his *right* to live. This unequivocally means that no one can ever give up a right. The only thing one may give up is the *specific possession* of what the right allows (meaning the specific Ferrari or Bob's life in and of itself). Giving up these specific possessions under natural law requires the person to voluntarily surrender them. Anyone who aggresses against somebody else, and forcibly takes possession of their property has broken the laws of nature. Since, in the case of capital punishment, no voluntary surrender of life has been given (and the right itself is incapable of being surrendered), then capital punishment absolutely violates the person's natural right to life.

The hard truth is that, despite the incredibly strong emotional argument behind the support of capital punishment, executing an unarmed person that is not an active threat against another individual is, without a doubt, murder. Even if the state sanctions and endorses the murder, be it at Konzentrationslager Auschwitz in Poland, or at the Texas State

Penitentiary in Huntsville, TX, it must be viewed the same as if sanctioned by a random individual.

Emotions are very powerful and are not easy to overcome. They are what drive many people to push for what always amounts to bad public policy. Many will dismiss this with ease given James Bigby's actions that led him to this point, but it is important to note that when he was strapped to the execution table on March 14, 2017, he was asked if he had any last words:

> *"Yes, I do, Grace Kehler is that you? I have given Warden Jones a written statement that will explain a lot more. I hope this will bring you closure and answers to some questions. I hope this will bring you peace and I'm sorry for all the pain and suffering. I'm sorry it went on for a terribly long time. I'm sorry to you especially Grace Kehler. To the Kehler, Johnson, and Crain family, I pray that you won't hate Jesus, the letter will explain more. I'm sorry. I'm sorry. I hope that my death will bring you peace and closure. I pray that maybe someday [it] will bring you peace. I hope that you could forgive me, but if you don't, I understand. I don't think I could forgive anyone who would have killed my children. I'm sorry for your suffering you've had for a long time. I'm sorry, I'm sorry. I love you Lord Jesus, Lord Jesus."*[94]

The sincerity of his last words will be speculated on from the time they were spoken until this entire event fades from history, but no one will ever be able to prove or disprove what was in his heart in those final moments. What is not up for speculation, however, is that he was immobilized on a table, injected with pentobarbital against his will, and his heart and brain function ceased fourteen minutes later.[95] Many advocates who oppose the death penalty cite the taxpayer costs associated with execution or bring up people who have been exonerated after being sentenced to death. These are all true talking points, but ultimately, they

---

94 Bagby, James Eugene (March 14, 2017). "Last Statement". Retrieved from https://www.tdcj.texas.gov/death_row/dr_info/bigbyjameslast.html
95 McCullough, Jolie. (March 14, 2017). "Texas Executes Fort Worth Man Who Killed a Father and an Infant". *The Texas Tribune*.

do not really matter. What matters is whether we believe that the right to live is a natural right. To say "I believe in the natural right to life, but…" means that you cannot believe that life is a natural right.

The same is true for the issue of gun rights. For the sake of ease, I will herein categorize everyone who support any gun control legislation under the umbrella term "gun controller," though I do recognize that those who support the full ban of all private firearm ownership are worlds apart from those who only support so-called "common sense gun safety laws" like background checks. Firearm ownership is undoubtedly a natural right, and the reason is because it is rooted in both our natural rights to life and property. While most on the pro-gun side will cite the 2nd Amendment to the United States Constitution, it ultimately does not matter whether the amendment even exists. Its only importance is that it was intended to serve as a prohibition against the state from infringing on it; however, this has proven to be only slightly effective to this end since 1934 with the adoption of the first federally enacted gun control law, the National Firearms Act.

Gun controllers are always motivated by the tragic loss of innocent life by an evil person using a firearm, and this is by no means something that should be dismissed. Victims of gun violence have had their lives robbed of them.. The victim's loved ones have also been robbed of the victim's life, as they will never again get to see or speak with them. It is certainly something with which any sane person can sympathize.

As cold as it may sound (and I do not mean this to be so), tragedy is not a valid reason to deprive any individual of their natural rights. Many gun controllers beg the nonsensical question of where nature provides us guns, or where religious scripture commands us to own the same. To answer it simply, every individual has the right to own whatever property he wishes and has the right to own whatever tools he deems necessary to defend his life and property from any outside aggressor.

When an evil person seeks to wreak havoc within a population, an unarmed individual will call someone with a firearm (e.g. the police) to come and neutralize the threat. What makes personal ownership of a firearm a natural right is a few simple facts: first, only the individual can be entrusted to take every action necessary to defend his own life. Law enforcement has zero legal duty to protect any individual, as mandated by numerous opinions issued by the U.S. Supreme Court, as well as lesser courts (see *Warren v. District of Columbia, Lozito v. New York City, De-Shaney v. Winnebago County,* and *Castle Rock v. Gonzales* as just a partial list). While most police officers will engage a threat on a private individual's behalf, should they not, they will face no legal repercussions for failing to do so. Furthermore, law enforcement is usually several minutes away in most cases, and in a scenario where even fractions of a second mean the difference between life and death, even their most heroic attempts will be in vain. To have this as the only means of individual protection, even with a legal mandate for first responders to defend individual life, effectively means that the individual is sentenced to death as law enforcement will never arrive on time.

Another reason the right to bear arms is a natural right is much more simplistic. Because property ownership is a natural right, nature places no stipulations or caveats on what type of property may be owned. If Bob machines a fully automatic belt-fed weapon in his garage, it is his property, and no one has the authority to tell him such property is illegal. If Bob sells that same weapon to John, the title of ownership is exchanged for a mutually agreed upon amount of money, and it rightfully becomes the property of John. Because of this fact, any law that controls or attempts to control the keeping and/or bearing of arms is a violation of the individual's right to property.

Many gun controllers also wonder where the arbitrary line is drawn for private ownership of various weapons. In the current political climate, the focus is on so-called "assault weapons," which is a euphemism for AR-15 and AK-47 platform weapons. In truth, there is no line to be drawn. Every individual has the right to make the determination for themselves what tools *they* deem necessary to adequately defend their lives, liberty, and property from those who seek to usurp it. Notice there is not a specification of an enemy. This is because any entity, even one's own government, may be an enemy for anyone. This is the very reason that one should have legal access to the same weaponry as the most powerful government on the planet.

Does this include nuclear weapons? Yes; however, there is one minor detail that conveniently gets overlooked when going to the extreme of fully militarized fighter jets and ICBMs. As I have previously outlined, capitalism requires both a supply and a demand to function. For private ownership of nuclear weapons to ever be a reality, there first must be a demand. A demand requires the ability to purchase, and for nuclear weapons, it is quite costly.

Based upon the lowest estimates for North Korea's nuclear development program, they have spent about $18 million per nuclear warhead, though this number varies wildly due to the classified nature of U.S. intelligence.[96] Assuming just that low-end price tag, the amount of people who could even afford one is incredibly small.

The definition of an "ultra-high net worth individual" is someone who has a net worth of over $30 million, and is currently comprised of just about 226,450 people, or 0.003% of the global population.[97] That is not enough of a population to justify a demand in any market, even if 100% of them actually wanted a nuclear weapon.

For the sake of argument, pretend that Jeff Bezos decided he wanted to purchase a nuclear weapon. He has the resources to do so, but for him to acquire one, he needs a willing seller. Since the U.S. hasn't manufactured a new nuclear warhead since the 1990s, there is quite literally zero supply. Capitalism alone would keep nuclear weapons and F-35s from being privately owned by any population, even if it were 100% legal to do so.

The other foundational argument for gun controllers is the idea that some people should be prohibited from owning or possessing firearms. Since 1968, there has been a codified list of "prohibited persons" that are unable to legally purchase a firearm from a Federal Firearms License (FFL) dealer. State laws have supplemented this federal law in order to penalize the mere possession of a firearm, and it has sadly been a welcome infringement by most Americans.

In October of 2019, a Slidell, Louisiana man named Hakim Dumas had an argument with his wife and took his son to a family member's house. His wife hired two men to kidnap the child, and Mr. Dumas

---

96 Blumberg, Yoni. (August 8, 2017). "Here's How Much a Nuclear Weapon Costs". *CNBC.*
97 Kenton, Will. (September 11, 2019). "Ultra-High Net Worth Individual (UHN-WI)". *Investopedia.*

defended his son with a firearm, killing one of the men and injuring the other. The sheriff's office admitted that it was a justified shooting and charged the surviving man, Billy Porche, with aggravated attempted kidnapping of a child, as well as second degree murder for the death of the man Mr. Dumas shot and killed.[98] Unfortunately, Hakim Dumas was a convicted felon, and the sheriff's office arrested him and charged him with felon in possession of a firearm, as well as possessing a firearm with an obliterated serial number. The felon in possession charge alone carries a penalty of 5 to 20 years in prison.

The fear that most people have with the idea of felons legally possessing firearms seems understandable on its face. Why would we *want* someone to possess a firearm who committed an act that violated another person's liberty? It is not an invalid question, but the answer is simply because they still have the right to do so. That said, there is plenty of data that shows that this "understandable" fear people have is based on a highly inflated perception of reality and is truly irrational.

In 2017, the University of Georgia published a study they conducted that estimated approximately 19 million Americans had a felony conviction on their record.[99] This number includes not only felons that were currently incarcerated and under a supervised status like parole but also felons that were fully integrated back into society. Using data from the Bureau of Justice Statistics, the overwhelming majority (about 75%) of incarcerated or supervised felons at both the state and federal levels were convicted of non-violent felony offenses. Breaking the data down to its base components, it shows that only about 1.07% of the U.S. population has a violent felony conviction and is *not* currently incarcerated or supervised.[100]

When the Hakim Dumas story was posted to social media, many inquired as to what his past felony conviction was, rationalizing that they would be okay with his possession of a firearm had it been non-violent.

---

98 Wills, Derek (October 28, 2019). "Father Faces Felony Charges After Shooting Two Men Attempting to Kidnap His Son." *Lone Star Gun Rights*.
99 Shannon, S.K.S., Uggen, C., Schnittker, J. et al. Demography (2017) 54: 1795. https://doi.org/10.1007/s13524-017-0611-1
100 Wills, Derek. (November 2, 2019). "Like it or Not, Felons Have the Right to Defend Their Lives... With Guns". *Lone Star Gun Rights*.

That question, however, does not matter. Even though it turned out that his past felony was drug-related, and there was no violent component attached to it, the question must be asked if it would change anything if it had. If he had been convicted of a homicide, for example, instead of drug offenses, would he have somehow lost his right to defend his son from being kidnapped? Not at all.

As a final point, it has been shown countless times that felons purchase black market firearms if they wish to arm themselves for either nefarious or noble reasons. Even in Mr. Dumas' case, he used a firearm with an obliterated serial number (i.e. a black market firearm) to defend his son. This ultimately proves that background checks, as well as laws prohibiting felons from possessing firearms are completely ineffective in achieving their intended goals. Not only are they ineffective, but they are unnecessary because the overall violent crime rate is incredibly low. In 2016, for example, only 0.114% of the population was the victim of a violent crime (aggravated assault, robbery, homicide, or rape) where their attacker used a firearm. [101]

Statistics like these are often met with the claim that the enacting of gun control is the clear reason as to why, but this is simply not the case. The year 1980 was the deadliest homicide year on record in the U.S. [102] with 23,039 homicides (14,386 of which were committed with a firearm). [103] With the population that year at 227.2 million, this means that 0.0063% were the victim of a homicide. That year, there were also 1,344,520 violent crimes committed, though no weapon data was included. [104] In 2016, about 31% of violent crimes were committed with a firearm. Assuming this percentage remained the same in 1980, this would mean that only 0.185% of Americans were the victims of violent crime committed with a firearm the same year that had the highest homicide rate in American history.

---

101 Crime in the United States, 2016. Retrieved from https://ucr.fbi.gov/crime-in-the-u.s/2016/crime-in-the-u.s.-2016/topic-pages/violent-crime. *Federal Bureau of Investigation.*
102 Key Facts at a Glance. Bureau of Justice Statistics. Retrieved from http://web.archive.org/web/20061024231800/http://www.ojp.usdoj.gov/bjs/glance/tables/hmrttab.htm
103 Homicide Trends in the United States, 1980–2008. Retrieved from https://www.bjs.gov/content/pub/pdf/htus8008.pdf
104 United States Crime Rates, 1960–2018. Retrieved from http://www.disastercenter.com/crime/uscrime.htm

A few things that must be noted for the year 1980:

- Background checks did not exist.
  - ○ These were fully implemented in 1998 following the signing of the Brady Handgun Violence Protection Act of 1993.
- Fully automatic weapons were only regulated by the National Firearms Act of 1934, requiring a $200 tax stamp and registration with the ATF.
  - ○ They were effectively banned with the signing of the Firearm Owners Protection Act of 1986.
- The prohibited persons provisions enacted by the Gun Control Act of 1968 were severely difficult to enforce without first arresting someone for the commission of a separate crime.
- Only 9 states really "allowed" the carrying of handguns in public.
  - ○ WA, ND, SD, IN, AL, CT, NH, and ME were "shall-issue" states, and VT was the only state without a licensing requirement.

The end goal for the average, everyday gun controller is to decrease the amount of cases where an innocent person becomes a victim of a violent crime committed with a firearm. A noble cause, to be sure, but the hard truth of the matter is that every single existing law has failed to achieve this end, and every future law will have the same result. To simplify their philosophy, they believe that controlling any or multiple aspects of firearm ownership will ultimately cut down on the number of times they are used to commit crimes, but this philosophy is fatally flawed.

Background checks, for example, are a great way to illustrate this point. There have been multiple cases where an evil person was able to pass a background check without any issues, and there is a very simple reason why. Background checks are just that: *back*ground checks. They are incapable of proving the future motives of any individual. If someone has never even been issued a parking ticket in their life, then even the most stringent background check system in the world will fail to flag him if his intentions were to commit a mass homicide. Likewise, a person with a felony conviction, like Hakim Dumas, could merely want to protect his family, but the infringement on his rights either force him to be a victim, or commit another criminal act by possessing the tools necessary to defend his son.

The motivations and goals behind why people support gun control are the same as those who believe that every single gun law is an infringement on our natural rights. The difference is the method to achieve that end. Gun controllers believe that law enforcement and legislation are effective methods to accomplish these goals, while gun rights absolutists believe that the only way to curb those who seek to invoke evil is to arm oneself.

While the gun controller philosophy sounds good on paper, in practice it is worthless. Criminals by their very definition do not follow the law. Those who seek to invoke evil will always find a way to do so, even if the firearm was magically obliterated from the face of the planet. Law enforcement has no legal duty to protect any of us, and even if they did, they are several minutes away at a time when fractions of a second mean the difference between life and death. The only answer to evil is to take personal responsibility for one's own security, and bear the tools necessary to fight evil from wherever it may come, including one's own government.

The mere possession of any weapon, be it an M2HB .50 caliber machine gun, an F-16 with a fully loaded 20mm Vulcan cannon, AIM-120D AMRAAMs, and AIM-9X Sidewinders, or even an ICBM does not infringe on any other individual's natural rights. While capitalism will essentially ensure that the latter two will not be possessed by the general public, society should not fear the private ownership of a belt-fed machine gun, or even handheld explosives, like frag grenades and flashbangs.

On April 19, 1775, when the British were defeated at Lexington and Concord, it was the private ownership of artillery (cannons) that helped aid the rebels in their victory. These were not licensed, nor were they illegal. They are the tools necessary for the preservation of liberty, and should be viewed as such.

If life is a natural right, how is it acceptable for someone to use a firearm in self-defense? Any act of aggression towards another is an act designed solely to place the victim into a state of slavery under him.

As touched on in Chapter 1, if an individual does not own themselves (their very lives being their rightful property), then they are owned by someone else, thus making them a slave. If an intruder violates your right to property by breaking into your home, they have in that very act aggressed against you, and attempted to make you their slave. Because they are proclaiming ownership of your tangible property, they have proven themselves capable of proclaiming ownership of your non-tangible property, including your very life. Therefore, for the sake of self-preservation and self-ownership, you must do what is necessary. Should this result in the cessation of their life, you cannot be held in violation of natural law, even though your actions did violate their natural right to life.

John Locke explained it thusly:

> *"[H]e who attempts to get another man into his absolute power, does thereby put himself into a state of war with him; it being to be understood as a declaration of a design upon his life: for I have reason to conclude, that he who would get me into his power without my consent, would use me as he pleased when he had got me there, and destroy me too when he had a fancy to it; for no body can desire to have me in his absolute power, unless it be to compel me by force to that which is against the right of my freedom, i.e. make me a slave. To be free from such force is the only security of my preservation; and reason bids me look on him, as an enemy to my preservation, who would take away that freedom which is the fence to it; so that he who makes an attempt to enslave me, thereby puts himself into a state of war with me. He that, in the state of nature, would take away the freedom that belongs to any one in that state, must necessarily be supposed to have a design to take away every thing else, that freedom being the foundation of all the rest; as he that, in the state of society, would take away the freedom belonging to those of that society or commonwealth, must be supposed to design to take away from them every thing else, and so be looked on as in a state of war.*
>
> *"This makes it lawful for a man to kill a thief, who has not in the least hurt him, nor declared any design upon his life, any farther than, by the use of force, so to get him in his power, as to take away*

his money, or what he pleases, from him; because using force, where he
has no right, to get me into his power, let his pretence be what it will,
I have no reason to suppose, that he, who would take away my liberty,
would not, when he had me in his power, take away every thing else.
And therefore it is lawful for me to treat him as one who has put him-
self into a state of war with me, i.e. kill him if I can; for to that hazard
does he justly expose himself, whoever introduces a state of war, and is
aggressor in it."[105]

There is, however, something that must be closely examined when it comes to matters of self-defense. The point at which the aggressor either surrenders or flees, using deadly force against him *would* constitute murder under natural law. The entire premise of self-defense is that it is purely a defensive form of aggression. Once an offensive aggressor surrenders or proves himself no longer an aggressor by fleeing, the act of shooting him ceases being a defensive act and becomes instead an offensive act of aggression. Similarly, any act of vengeance would also be an act of offensive aggression. For example, if John had sexually assaulted Sally, a heinous crime indeed, should Sally approach John after a period of time and kill him, she has aggressed against him from an offensive posture, and thus such act of vengeance would constitute a murder under natural law.

It is important to reiterate that self-defense, by its very definition, must be practiced from a defensive posture. Such a posture can only exist when a person is actively aggressing against you. If a thief upon being discovered flees, even with some of your property, he has proven his intentions are not to take possession of your life. In such a circumstance, therefore, while he has commit*ted* an act of aggression against you by means of theft, the moment he flees, he is no longer commit*ting* an act of aggression against you, and thus killing him would constitute murder.

Finally, how does this relate to a literal state of war, for instance, during a revolutionary uprising? Despite war's complexity, this is quite a simple answer. When the state becomes tyrannical, as it invariably does, it is logically no different than a person who aggresses against an individual. The difference is that when the state does it, it does so in a constant

---

105 Locke, John. (1689). *"Second Treatise of Government"*. Chapter III.

position of passive offensive aggression towards those it believes to be its slaves. Because of this, the right of the people to rise up against, and subsequently overthrow their government is not a violation of natural law. It should be noted, however, that the premeditation of revolution must be carried out when direct, active hostilities are presented from the state. For example, it is a violation of natural law to begin a revolution with the preemptive bombing of a government building. Such an act would invoke casualties of noncombatants. Though there are likely several appropriate ways to revolt against one's oppressive state, one proper way, for example, would be to refuse to have your taxes withheld, and subsequently refuse to file them. Once audits are ignored for a substantial amount of time, the state will certainly send combatants to invoke violence against the individual. At that point, the state has taken up armed hostilities against them. During war, any aggression shown towards any noncombatant, or even a surrendered combatant, would be a violation of natural law.

Chapter 7

The Injustice System

"Where justice is denied, where poverty is enforced, where ignorance prevails, and where any one class is made to feel that society is an organized conspiracy to oppress, rob and degrade them, neither persons nor property will be safe." – Frederick Douglass

L iberty and justice are typically thought of as going hand-in-hand. After all, the Pledge of Allegiance closes by saying "with liberty and justice for all," and the very fabric of the American culture rests on a foundation of combatting the historical injustices that led to our revolutionary ideals. Indeed, justice is quintessential to liberty. Today, however, Lady Justice has been removed from her pedestal, and tyranny has taken her place.

Justice is blind, which is why she has always been depicted blindfolded holding a scale and a sword. The idea is that no matter one's status, from the elite politician to the lowly peasant, everyone is treated and tried with impartiality. They are supposed to be presumed innocent until proven guilty. Unfortunately, however, today's "justice" system is not worthy of such a label, as it implies some semblance of justice exists.

The maxim that "it is better that ten guilty persons escape than that one innocent suffer" is attributed to English jurist William Blackstone from his 1770 work, *Commentaries on the Laws of England* (though the idea itself dates back to even religious scriptures). In Blackstone's writing, he said:

> *"[A]ll presumptive evidence of felony should be admitted cautiously: for the law holds, that it is better that ten guilty persons escape, than that one innocent suffer. And Sir Matthew Hale in particular lays down two rules, most prudent and necessary to be observed: 1. Never to convict a man for stealing the goods of a person unknown, merely because*

he will give no account how he came by them, unless an actual felony be proved of such goods: and, 2. Never to convict any person of murder or manslaughter, till at least the body be found dead; on account of two instances he mentions, where persons were executed for the murder of others, who were then alive, but missing."[106]

The full understanding of this doctrine is essential to the preservation (and restoration) of liberty. Words have very specific meanings, and in today's America, the very vocabulary with which common phrases are made up have lost their true definitions. The word "justice" has had its meaning bastardized from its philosophical roots as the means of making whole a victim whose natural rights were violated. Today, it has been reduced to merely being a euphemism for the enforcement and execution of "the law." "Law and order" has become synonymous with justice's philosophical attributes, and when the politician claims he is "tough on crime," he is admitting nothing more than support for laws that would turn an otherwise innocent person into a guilty one.

The bigger issue, however, is the presumption that the law and justice are interchangeable. Only in times of political debate are specific laws brought under scrutiny of being unjust, and the partisan talking points only cheapen the validity of the real grievance.

Benjamin Franklin is often quoted as one of the sources for Blackstone's doctrine due to a letter he wrote in 1785. What gets omitted from Franklin's letter, however, is what immediately follows, which is arguably more important:

"That it is better 100 guilty Persons should escape, than that one innocent Person should suffer, is a Maxim that has been long and generally approv'd, never that I know of controverted. Even the sanguinary Author of the Thoughts [on Executive Justice] agrees to it [on] page 163, adding well, that 'the very Thought of injured Innocence, and much

---

106 Blackstone, William. (1770). *"Commentaries on the Laws of England."* Book the Fourth: Of Public Wrongs; Chapter the Twenty-Seventh: Of Trial, and Conviction. Retrieved from https://avalon.law.yale.edu/subject_menus/blackstone.asp

more that of suffering Innocence, must awaken all our tenderest and most compassionate Feelings, and at the same time raise our highest Indignation against the Instruments of it.' But, he adds, 'there is no Danger of either from a strict Adherence to the Laws.' Really? Is it then impossible to make an unjust Law? And if the Law itself be unjust, may it not be the very 'Instrument' which ought to 'raise the Author's, and every body's, highest Indignation.'"[107]

The assumption that most laws are just is an egregious error that is incredibly common, and it is almost entirely responsible for the current state of society. It has created a semi-totalitarian state that has all but destroyed the justice system. What exists in its stead is merely a legal system designed to execute the arbitrary will of the government machine.

The United States is still known as the land of the free, yet this is an incredibly ironic label when one considers that we have the highest incarceration rate in the world.[108] The company with which we share the top 10 spots is something to behold as well (rates per 100,000):

1. United States of America – 655[109]
2. El Salvador – 604
3. Turkmenistan – 552
4. Virgin Islands (USA) – 542
5. Thailand – 529
6. Rwanda – 511
7. Cuba – 510
8. Maldives – 499
9. Northern Mariana Islands (USA) – 482
10. Virgin Islands (United Kingdom) – 470

107 Franklin, Benjamin (March 14, 1785). To Benjamin Vaughan. Retrieved from https://franklinpapers.org/yale;jsessionid=node01djdmkozc200w15jkq48jr-40wp1161805.node0?d=-28187442&vol=42&page=712
108 Highest to Lowest – Prison Population Rate. World Prison Brief. Retrieved from https://www.prisonstudies.org/highest-to-lowest/prison_population_rate?field_region_taxonomy_tid=All
109 NOTE: Incarceration rate includes pre-trial detainees, local jail population, Indian Country jails, and juvenile facilities. U.S. incarceration rate would be 580 per 100,00 if those figures were excluded.

In 2016, there were approximately 4.5 million people on probation or parole[110], 1.5 million inmates in federal and state prisons[111], and local jails had an average daily population of 731,300 people.[112] In total, over 6.7 million people were part of the criminal "justice" system in the United States, or 2.7% of the total adult population. This, however, does not tell the entire story. The question must be raised as to why nearly 3% of 251 million adults are being prosecuted by the state.

We first must determine what constitutes a criminal act before we can break down the data. If liberty's definition is to be strictly adhered to when it comes to criminal acts, then such acts require the existence of a victim. Drug offenses would not meet this criterion; and yes, this means *all* drugs. This statement is invariably met with revulsion, as many wrongfully equate the support for the legalization of drugs to an endorsement of their use; however, this is a habit that must be broken if we are to restore liberty. We must apply the adage of "I disapprove of what you say, but I will defend to the death your right to say it" in every aspect, and though we may disapprove of what an individual *does*, we should defend to the death their right to do it.

Opioids are incredibly destructive for an addict, and the chemical drive behind the addiction to drugs like heroin has been fatal for many. The tragedy of opioid use is not one to be glossed over, as this affects real people who are dealing with demons unique to them. The reason these drugs are controlled so strictly by the state is because of that very fact. The problem, however, is the attempt to control in and of itself.

Aside from the fact that the urge for the state to control opiates and cocaine was entirely rooted in racism,[113] the attempts have done exactly nothing positive to solve the problem. In 1909, a report was published by the International Opium Commission in Shanghai that estimated the total addiction rate for opioids in the United States to be

---

110 Kaeble, Danielle. (April 2018). "Probation and Parole in the United States, 2016". *Bureau of Justice Statistics*.
111 Carson, E. Ann. (January 2018). "Prisoners in 2016". *Bureau of Justice Statistics*.
112 Zeng, Zhen. (February 2018). "Jail Inmates in 2016". *Bureau of Justice Statistics*.
113 Williams, Edward Huntington, M.D. (February 8, 1914). "Negro Cocaine 'Fiends' New Southern Menace". *New York Times*.

0.18% among the adult population.[114] Today, it is estimated to be over 1% of the adult population, with about 77% of those being addicted to medications prescribed by a doctor. An estimated 591,000 (0.24% of the adult population) are addicted to heroin specifically.[115]

The prohibition and control of narcotics have only led to even more detrimental consequences than before the state's involvement. First and foremost, such controls only create a black market, which is simply a representation of the real free market. Any market seeks survival, which is why companies make necessary changes to adapt as the market dictates. For black markets, the need to survive requires the incitement of violence.

The best illustration of this was the alcohol prohibition era in the United States. Both before and after prohibition, bar owners, brewers, and spirit distillers never violently attacked their competition because the free and open market was the driving force behind their survival. During prohibition, however, violence spread between competitors, as well as to law enforcement trying to shut them down. The easiest explanation for this is simply because the state inherently uses the threat of violence in order to enforce their laws. Should a cop have happened upon a moonshiner, he would have demanded the distiller come with him to be locked up, and his property used to distill the alcohol would be destroyed. Refusing such a demand means the cop must use force (violence) in order to fulfill his goal of an arrest, and the use of deadly force is always an option if he were to attempt to defend himself from the kidnapping attempt (arrest). Because the state's inherent threat of deadly force against someone breaking their laws is ever present, the need for a black market to survive requires it to be prepared to meet that threat with the same level of force.

Alcohol prohibition did not rid the nation of alcoholics, and drug prohibition has not rid the nation of addicts. Not only is violence perpetuated by the mere existence of prohibition, but the black market is not able

---

114 Wright, Hamilton. (1909). *Report of the International Opium Commission, Shanghai, China, February 1 to February 26, 1909*
115 Opioid Addiction 2016 Facts and Figures. *American Society of Addiction Medicine.* Retrieved from https://www.asam.org/docs/default-source/advocacy/opioid-addiction-disease-facts-figures.pdf

to control the aspects of the products like it would in an open and free market. Because of this, the end user is receiving a product far more dangerous to him than he would have otherwise had access to. A black market is far more volatile than an open market, as production and distribution (the supply) is always at risk of a sudden drop due to law enforcement efforts. This causes black market narcotics dealers to cut their products with worse chemicals, such as rat poison, drywall, or other easily obtainable cutting agents. Furthermore, the production process itself will likely produce impurities that would not otherwise be present in an open market product.

What has resulted from all of this is senseless deaths of drug addicts and law enforcement, as well as the ruining of various lives who either never actually harmed anyone, or would not have harmed anyone had the threat of violence from the state not existed. Cory Jay was a father of three children, a boyfriend, a brother, and a son. He was also addicted to methamphetamine. On August 1, 2019, Cory was driving his motorcycle in Oklahoma City, OK when law enforcement attempted to pull him over for a traffic violation. Cory's addiction had landed him a prior arrest, and on this day, he was on probation. He was also in possession of methamphetamine. Instead of pulling over, Cory panicked and sped off knowing that getting caught with the drugs on him would ensure he would not see his children for a very long time. The pursuit ended when Cory lost control of his motorcycle, struck the wall of the freeway, and "fell 20 to 30 feet from the bridge after he hit the barrier."[116] Cory's obituary painted a beautiful picture describing the man he was:

> *"Cory had many friends as he took people for who they were, not who he thought they should be. He was someone a friend could always count on and one who would always tell you the truth, even if you didn't want to hear it…he was a straight shooter! He enjoyed and was very talented artistically. He loved to randomly sketch things and his dream was to become a tattoo artist. Most importantly Cory just enjoyed spending time with his kids… Those were the times he lived for."[117]*

116 Pierce, Jennifer (August 2, 2019). "Motorcyclist Dies After Striking Wall, Ejected Over Bridge in OKC High-Speed Chase". *News 9*.
117 "Obituary". *Buchanan Funeral Service* (https://www.buchananfuneralservice.com/obituary/cory-jay). Cory Alan Jay of Oklahoma City, Oklahoma | 1988-2019

Cory never violated the liberty of anyone yet was made into a criminal for his flaws. Had narcotics never been controlled by the state, Cory would still be alive today. His three children would still have their father, and his parents would still have their son. Instead, Cory's life was abruptly ended at age 31 because the threat of imprisonment by the state forced him to make a choice he never should have had to make.

Ending the drug war would have massive benefits for everyone involved. Law enforcement would not be put into nearly as many needlessly dangerous situations, thus reducing the risks they face of not coming home to their families. Drug dealers would be replaced simply by pharmaceutical entrepreneurs, and because an open market would exist, violence would not occur for its survival. Addicts, recreational, and medicinal users would all have the means to set potency and purity standards, thus reducing their intake of chemicals more toxic than the drug itself (and yes, there are medicinal uses for drugs like methamphetamine, psilocybin mushrooms, and even fentanyl). All of this aside, the true benefit of a free and open market for narcotics is the treatment of addicts as human beings with a disease instead of dehumanizing them as criminals needing to be locked in a cage. Not only have similar policies led to a massive reduction in addiction rates, overdoses, and the spread of diseases in countries like Portugal,[118] but those battling addiction do not deserve to have their problems treated criminally.

Of the over 6 million people incarcerated or on parole mentioned earlier, over 73% of them were convicted of non-violent drug offenses. If drug crimes were all eliminated, the federal and state prison population would decrease by over half (to 716,480 from 1,459,533), and the supervised population would decrease by over 80% (to 886,864 from 4,547,897). Assuming no change to the daily average local jail population, the 2.7% of the adult population involved in the criminal "justice" system in 2016 would have been reduced to merely 0.9%. There is no way to know what percentage of violent felons only committed those acts of violence due to drug prohibition, but it is likely that the number of violent felons would decrease substantially as well.

---

118 Ferreira, Susana. (December 5, 2017). "Portugal's Radical Drugs Policy is Working. Why Hasn't the World Copied It?". *The Guardian*.

There is another major problem with the legal system, even when it is a legitimate criminal act being tried: sentencing. First, sentencing in no way brings any retribution to the victim. The focus is on punishing the guilty individual for his transgressions. The purpose of justice is to fairly redress grievances for a victim, but sending the guilty individual into exile does not do anything to achieve that end. Since the trauma experienced by a victim of a heinous crime or the loss of a loved one is not corrected in any way, a simple sentence of exile, even one for the rest of their life, in no way creates any notion of justice being served.

The other major fallacy is that legislative guidelines for minimum sentencing fail to take semantic details of the crime into account, and thus ensures that many guilty individuals will become victims of the state. Similar to how we rightfully view premeditated murder to be more severe of a crime than a murder committed as a result of negligence or insanity, not all first-degree murder cases are created equally. Mandating sentencing minimums by law forces judges to ignore circumstances that should justly result in a lesser sentence.

Giving full discretion to judges does not solve this issue either. Several sentencing guidelines set minimums relatively low in order to give judges more discretion to account for those circumstances, but this has also led to negative consequences. In 2017, a report was published by the United States Sentencing Commission updating previous reports dating back to 2010. In it, the USSC highlights that "Black male offenders received sentences on average 19.1 percent longer than similarly situated white male offenders."[119] While this is a travesty that is commonly cited by advocates of justice reform, what gets overlooked is the discrepancies between men and women.

In the Key Findings summary of the report, while it made a point to highlight the 19.1% longer sentences given to black males compared to white males, it only mentioned that "[t]he differences in sentence length [between male and female offenders] decreased slightly," ignoring the fact that the discrepancies were much larger than that between

---

119 Schmitt, Glenn R., Reedt, Louis, and Blackwell, Kevin. (November 2017). "Demographic Differences in Sentencing: An Update to the 2012 Booker Report". *United States Sentencing Commission.*

races. The report found the following when compared to sentences of white males:[120]

- White females – 28.9% shorter
- Black females – 29.7% shorter
- Hispanic females – 16.8% shorter
- Other females – 35.4% shorter

Considering that black males were sentenced to 19.1% longer sentences than that of white males, it is not difficult to calculate that black males were sentenced to 69.4% longer sentences than black females for similar crimes, and white males were sentenced to 40.6% longer sentences than white females. To put this into perspective, should a white male have been sentenced to 10 years in prison, a black male would be sentenced to nearly 12 years, and a black female would be sentenced to barely 7 years for the exact same crime. A white female would serve about a month longer than the black female.

Sentencing an individual to prison does nothing to even attempt to make the victim whole again. Judges have demonstrated that they cannot be trusted with fair sentencing between races and sexes, and legislation cannot account for the important semantics surrounding why a crime was committed. Considering these realities, how can society ensure that justice is fair? It is a daunting question to say the least, and one that needs to be answered. While the state's supposed purpose is to ensure the application of fair justice, what is the mechanism that ensures the state's application of justice remains fair? Many would contend that it is the people that have the duty to keep the state in check, but this has proven to be ineffective at best. This question will be answered in Part II.

---

120 Schmitt, Reedt, and Blackwell. (2017). *United States Sentencing Commission.*

Chapter 8

Immigration & Naturalization

"The bosom of America is open to receive not only the opulent and respectable Stranger, but the oppressed and persecuted of all Nations and Religions..." - George Washington

One of the most triggering topics in politics today is undoubtedly the issue of immigration. While it has certainly had its time in and out of the spotlight over recent decades, the current times have placed the issue front and center. This is largely due to Donald Trump's speech announcing his candidacy for president in June of 2015:

> *"When Mexico sends its people, they're not sending their best. They're not sending you. They're not sending you. They're sending people that have lots of problems, and they're bringing those problems with us [sic]. They're bringing drugs. They're bringing crime. They're rapists. And some, I assume, are good people."*[121]

When one pairs these sentiments with tragic news reports, such as the murder of Kate Steinle in July of 2015, it is easy to see why people buy into the narrative that immigration is something that needs to be strictly controlled by the state for the purpose of public safety at the very least. Donald Trump won his presidential bid in 2016 because of his push to implement such controls, which included building a wall on the southern border. Conservatives and Republicans (and others) who believe in border security do so because they believe it is essential to the preservation of liberty. After all, terrorists want to kill us, drug cartels are invoking violence

---

121 Time Staff (June 16, 2015). "Here's Donald Trump's Presidential Announcement Speech". *Time.*

in our country, many migrants are reaping government benefits, and lest we forget, they are taking our jobs. What gets lost in all of this propaganda, however, is that controlling immigration is actually *antithetical* to liberty.

Think about the word "liberty" for a moment. It does seem a little out of place among the other natural rights of life and property when you stop to really ponder on it. There is a general understanding of what life and property are, as they are very concrete ideas. The fact that the first chapter of this book needed to be written is indicative of the fact that "liberty" is far more abstract of an idea than life and property are. If you were to take the definition of liberty and reduce it down to its lowest common denominator, understanding our natural rights is very simple. We have the natural right to be alive (life), freely make our own choices (liberty), and own the fruits of our labor (property). Controlling immigration is antithetical to liberty because by forbidding or even encroaching upon the relocation of an individual emigrating from his birthplace, his natural right to live his life is violated, regardless of whether his purpose for relocating is due to tyranny. We would no doubt get up in arms about a law that required the government's approval for us to move across state lines.

I know these sentiments will not garner any favor from those who oppose the idea of open immigration, as many on the political right tout the idea of open borders as a dangerous one, but as Jefferson said, "I prefer dangerous liberty to peaceful servitude." What is truly ironic about this subject is that conservatives will always cry out about restoring the America that our Founding Fathers built, but they seem to be very ignorant of the fact that the United States of America had open borders for the first century of our existence, and those first laws were legitimately rooted in a disgusting discrimination against people who were not white men. It is not lost on me that such a statement in our current political climate is usually dismissed instantly, as the overwhelming majority of cries about viewpoints being racist/sexist/bigoted/homophobic are absolutely baseless, but in truth, it wasn't until 1965 that the foundation of our current immigration policy was laid.

Following the ratification of the U.S. Constitution in 1787, the 1st Congress sought to "establish a uniform Rule of Naturalization" per Article I § 8, and passed the Naturalization Act of 1790. This act established such uniformity in that "any alien, being a free white person," could become a citizen provided they had been a resident of the United States for at least two years, and "making proof to the satisfaction of such court"[122] of their residency. In 1795, the 3rd Congress amended these requirements to a 5-year residency and added the requirement that the person had declared "three years, at least, before his admission, that it was bona fide, his intention to become a citizen of the United States."[123] These were again amended in 1798 to a 14-year residency and a 5-year notification, but these were restored back to the 1795 requirements in 1802.

Despite all this back and forth, exactly none of these laws ever touched the issue of immigration, only naturalization. While these two issues seem to get blurred, they are very different. Immigration is a simple relocation, whereas naturalization is the act of an immigrant becoming a citizen of their new country.

Naturalization laws saw very little change from 1802 until 1870, when Congress extended the citizenship laws to include "aliens of African nativity, and to persons of African descent."[124] It wasn't until the passage of the Page Act in 1875, ninety-nine years after America's founding, that the first law controlling immigration into the United States was passed. Following the Civil War, an influx of immigrants from Asian countries (mainly China) began to concern the U.S. government, as their customs seemed incredibly different to that of white Europeans. This prompted fear and propaganda from vocal politicians, who sought to find a way to stop these particular foreigners from entering the country.

During this time, prostitution was perfectly legal at the state and federal levels, but California Republican Congressman, Horace Page, decided to use the issue of prostitution to close the borders to Asian immigrants. Despite the fact that the overwhelming majority of Asian immigrants were

122 *An Act to establish a uniform Rule of Naturalization.* (March 26, 1790). 1 Stat. 103. Retrieved from https://govtrackus.s3.amazonaws.com/legislink/pdf/stat/1/STAT-UTE-1-Pg103.pdf
123 *An Act to establish a uniform rule of Naturalization; and to repeal the act heretofore passed on that subject.* (January 29, 1795). 1 Stat. 414. Retrieved from https://govtrackus.s3.amazonaws.com/legislink/pdf/stat/1/STATUTE-1-Pg414a.pdf
124 *An Act to amend the Naturalization Laws and to punish Crimes against the same, and for other Purposes.* (July 14, 1870). 16 Stat. 254. Retrieved from https://govtrackus.s3.amazonaws.com/legislink/pdf/stat/16/STATUTE-16-Pg254a.pdf

male, Page thought that targeting Asian women would curb the number of men entering. The act forbade "any subject of China, Japan, or any Oriental country" from entering the United States "for lewd and immoral purposes." It went on to clarify that "it shall be unlawful for aliens of the following classes to immigrate into the United States, namely... women imported for the purposes of prostitution."[125] To help sell this as a need for the federal government to control, propaganda backed by the American Medical Association insinuated the notion that "Chinese immigrants carried distinct germs to which they were immune, but from which whites could die if exposed."[126] The Page Act went on to be signed into law by President Grant on March 3, 1875, and officially ended open borders in the United States.

The plan, however, did not achieve the desired outcome. Instead, a new "problem" surfaced that seemed to threaten American whites. Asian men continued to immigrate into the United States, and "since there was a shortage of Chinese women, many of them either patronized white prostitutes or set up small brothels and hired them; others married or cohabited with working-class white women."[127] In 1882, Congressman Page sought to solve this "problem" once and for all.

In what history has appropriately dubbed the Chinese Exclusion Act, Horace Page authored a new law that made it unlawful "for any Chinese laborer to come, or... to remain within the United States" and "any Chinese person found unlawfully within the United States shall be caused to be removed therefrom to the country from whence he came." To add even more salt to the wound, the act also stipulated that "no State court or court of the United States shall admit Chinese to citizenship."[128] The act did include a sunset provision set to expire after ten years, however, California Democrat Thomas Geary renewed it in 1892.

125 *An act supplementary to the acts in relation to immigration.* (March 3, 1875). 18 Stat. 477. Retrieved from https://govtrackus.s3.amazonaws.com/legislink/pdf/stat/18/STATUTE-18-Pg477.pdf
126 Luibheid, E., Luibhéid, E. (2002). Entry Denied: Controlling Sexuality at the Border. United Kingdom: *University of Minnesota Press.*
127 McNeill, Maggie. (April 2012). "A Brief History of Prostitution in the US". *The Honest Courtesan.*
128 *An act to execute certain treaty stipulations relating to Chinese.* (May 6, 1882). 22 Stat. 58. Retrieved from https://govtrackus.s3.amazonaws.com/legislink/pdf/stat/22/STATUTE-22-Pg58c.pdf

Not only did the Geary Act renew Page's 1882 provisions, but it also instituted the precursor to today's "green card." The law established a "certificate of residence" that, if an Asian immigrant was found "without such certificate of residence, shall be deemed and adjudged to be unlawfully within the United States." It is also important to note that even though the aforementioned Acts since 1882 stipulate "Chinese," this was understood to mean all Asian immigrants under that umbrella term, as evidenced by the following from the law:

> *"SEC. 2. That any Chinese person or person of Chinese descent, when convicted and adjudged under any of said laws to be not lawfully entitled to be or remain in the United States, shall be removed from the United States to China, unless… he or they are subjects or citizens of some other country, in which case he or they shall be removed from the United States to such country."*[129]

Though the Geary Act also contained a 10-year sunset, all of these egregious provisions were made permanent in 1902. Congress then began really buckling down on the topic of immigration with new laws being enacted more frequently, which became less about race and more about eugenics. In 1903, Congress prohibited the immigration of "idiots, insane persons, epileptics… polygamists, anarchists"[130] and others. In 1907, "imbeciles, feeble-minded persons…, [and] physically defective"[131] persons were added to the list of excluded people. In 1917, Congress added prohibitions for immigrants "who are natives of islands not possessed by the United States adjacent to the Continent of Asia."[132]

---

129 *An act to prohibit the coming of Chinese persons into the United States.* (May 5, 1892). 27 Stat. 25. Retrieved from https://govtrackus.s3.amazonaws.com/legislink/pdf/stat/27/STATUTE-27-Pg25.pdf

130 *An act to regulate the immigration of aliens into the United States.* (March 3, 1903). 32 Stat. 1213. Retrieved from https://govtrackus.s3.amazonaws.com/legislink/pdf/stat/32/STATUTE-32-Pg1213.pdf

131 *An Act To regulate the immigration of aliens into the United States.* (February 20, 1907). 34 Stat. 898. Retrieved from https://govtrackus.s3.amazonaws.com/legislink/pdf/stat/34/STATUTE-34-Pg898.pdf

132 *An Act To regulate the immigration of aliens to, and the residence of aliens in, the United States.* (February 5, 1917). 39 Stat. 874. Retrieved from https://govtrackus.s3.amazonaws.com/legislink/pdf/stat/39/STATUTE-39-Pg874a.pdf

Finally, in 1924, the disgusting foundation for these immigration restrictions came full circle. Congress established the Eugenics Committee of the United States Committee on Selective Immigration to be the entity which reported on the new immigration bill. Three years earlier, Congress established the first quota system for immigration, and it was the job of the Eugenics Committee to report on how the new bill would impact the nation.

Harry Laughlin was a leading expert on the topic of eugenics and was appointed as an "expert eugenics agent" to the Eugenics Committee. (He was also an advocate for compulsory sterilization legislation and would later create models used by Nazi Germany in 1933 for their efforts of ensuring that 350,000 people couldn't pollute the Arian race). In the report released by the Committee, Congress utilized Laughlin's expertise in stating that the Immigration Act of 1924 would "greatly reduce the number of immigrants of the lower grades of intelligence, and of immigrants who are making excessive contribution to our feebleminded, insane, criminal, and other socially inadequate classes."[133] Despite this, Laughlin was not fully satisfied with the bill as he wanted it to do more, stating "our future laws, if the country is to be protected against inferior immigrants and is to select and welcome superior strains, should provide by statute for the determination of individual and hereditary qualities by requiring modern pedigree examination in the home territories of the would-be immigrant."[134]

Following the 1924 Act's passage, Congress continued to tweak and revise immigration laws every few years. It wasn't until 1943, a full 68 years since the passage of the Page Act, that immigrants from Asian nations could finally begin immigrating to the United States again and be eligible for citizenship. The repeal, however, wasn't in full, as prohibitions against property ownership by Asian immigrants (and Asian U.S. citizens) still existed at the state and federal levels. It also undercut the number of Asian immigrants allowed by the quota system revised by the 1924 Act by about 95%. The quota should have allowed for

---

133 *An Act To regulate the immigration of aliens into the United States.* (February 20, 1907). 34 Stat. 898. (1907).
134 Baynton, D. C. (2016). Defectives in the Land: Disability and Immigration in the Age of Eugenics. *University of Chicago Press.*

2,150 immigrants from China, but only 105 immigrants were granted entry.[135]

The first steps toward ending discrimination in the nation's immigration policy came in 1952. In 1965, the complete abolition of the quota system, as well as the remaining discriminatory laws against Asian immigrants that had been in effect for 90 years, finally established the basis for today's immigration policy.

While today's immigration policies are not aimed at an immigrant's race per se, the propaganda being spewed is little different than that of 1875. I do not believe that most people who want controlled immigration are bigoted in their motivations. What is clearly evident, however, is these controls are desired out of fear. As Donald Trump said in 2015, "They're bringing drugs. They're bringing crime. They're rapists." As president, he also pushed the point that Muslim prayer rugs had been found at the border.[136] All of these points are fear-based, leaving the population screaming for the illusion of security.

As mentioned earlier, President Trump's plan to stop illegal immigration was centered around a wall on the southern border. The big problem with this is that most undocumented immigrants in the United States entered the country lawfully, but overstayed their visa. According to a 2019 report by the Center for Migration Studies, "Of the estimated 515,000 arrivals in 2016, a total of 320,000, or 62 percent, were overstays…"[137] leaving the remainder being unlawful crossings. To the point of Muslim terrorism, it is worth noting that the September 11 hijackers were lawfully in the U.S. on student visas.

Regardless of the means of entry, the claim that the undocumented immigrant population is inherently more dangerous is a blatant lie. According to a July 2018 report from the Government Accountability Office (GAO), there were 27.1 million aliens in the United States, of which

---

135 "Comparison of Asian Populations During the Exclusion Years". Retrieved from https://www1.udel.edu/readhistory/resources/2005_2006/summer_06/hsu.pdf

136 Oprysko, Caitlin. (January 18, 2019). "Trump Touts Story About Finding 'Prayer Rugs' Along Border". *Politico*.

137 Warren, Robert. (January 16, 2019). "US Undocumented Population Continued to Fall from 2016 to 2017, and Visa Overstays Significantly Exceeded Illegal Crossings for the Seventh Consecutive Year". *Center for Migration Studies*.

approximately 12.1 million (44.6%) were in the country unlawfully.[138] When comparing federal convictions between U.S. citizens and the alien population, the data shows that per capita, the number of "bad guys" is essentially the same between the two populations.

Take the claim that "they're rapists" as an example. According to the GAO report, there were 2,445 U.S. citizens and 110 aliens federally convicted of sex offenses in 2016. When comparing these numbers to their respective populations, that accounts for 0.0011% of adult citizens, and 0.0005% of adult aliens respectively. It is important to note that the report does not differentiate between the statuses of the aliens being convicted. Should 100% of the aliens convicted been in the country unlawfully, then 0.0012% of the undocumented population were convicted of federal sex offenses. Clearly, the claim that "they're rapists" is unfounded.

There are only two areas where the number of alien convictions is disproportionate to the number of citizen convictions: drug crimes and immigration crime. As discussed in the previous chapter, drug crimes should not exist, and it is unsurprising that the alien population is disproportionately convicted of immigration crimes. If all of the convictions of victimless crimes were eliminated, then the percentage of federal convictions by aliens drops from 42% to 12%.

It is also worth mentioning the State Criminal Alien Assistance Program (SCAAP), which reimburses states for prosecuting undocumented aliens for state crimes. As has been previously discussed, state governments never miss out on an opportunity for federal tax dollars, and SCAAP is no different. While data on the number of undocumented aliens convicted or incarcerated in state facilities is unavailable, the total number of SCAAP reimbursements in 2015 was 169,300. Of those, according to the GAO report, "66 percent occurred in seven states—California, Texas, Florida, Arizona, New Jersey, New York, and Illinois." The difficulty in dialing in the data on state convictions is due to the fact that an undocumented alien "could have multiple

138 "Criminal Alien Statistics: Information on Incarcerations, Arrests, Convictions, Costs, and Removals" (July 2018). *Government Accountability Office*. Retrieved from https://www.gao.gov/assets/700/693162.pdf

SCAAP incarcerations during the reporting period." What can be concluded, however, is that the number of incarcerations into state prisons is substantially low. New York, for example, had 51,744 prison inmates in 2015, 89.6% of which were born in the United States.[139] This ultimately proves that undocumented immigrants are no more dangerous than natural born citizens.

Aside from the fear of the "criminal element" within the undocumented population, many on the political right believe that undocumented immigrants receive a significant amount of government benefits, a grievance which is not entirely unfounded. Per U.S. law, undocumented aliens are not legally allowed to receive government benefits; however, there are numerous reports of fraudulent claims being made about the use of fake documentation being used to garner such benefits, with some estimates being north of $100 billion annually.[140] Though this estimate is likely very high, the foundational issue is no doubt a problem. This problem, however, is not one with immigration; it is a problem with the redistribution of wealth.

Simply put, many believe the same propaganda that's being pushed by media outlets today that was being pushed back in the 1870s. They support controls on immigration out of fear, but fear is not a valid reason to infringe on anyone's liberty. In fact, fear is the very reason liberty needs to be protected.

The common talking point among conservatives is the claim that a country which does not control immigration is somehow not a country. This claim is bogus, as the history of our own nation proves. It would be the same as saying that Alabama isn't really a state because it allows non-Alabama residents to enter and exit the state without any controls.

What truly hammers home this misguided belief in the need for controlled entry into a country is the requirement for passports to travel

---

139 Dworakowski, Kim (April 2016). "Profile of Under Custody Population as of January 1, 2016". *New York State | Corrections and Community Supervision*. Retrieved from https://doccs.ny.gov/system/files/documents/2019/09/UnderCustody_Report_2016.pdf
140 La Jeunesse, William (April 22, 2019) "Most Illegal Immigrants in US Receive Government Benefits, Costing Taxpayers Billions: Experts". *Fox News*.
"NOLA Border Patrol Arrests 15 Illegal Aliens Caught Using Fake Documents". (August 19, 2019). *U.S. Customs and Border Protection*.

abroad. Everyone alive today is conditioned to believe this to be the norm even though it is a relatively new requirement. Though passports have existed for thousands of years, the use of passports were used as a means of controlling the *internal* travel of a king's subjects. Whether it was a king's servant issued a passport to effectively indicate he wasn't a runaway slave, or only issued if a peasant's taxes were paid, the passport always served as a subject's permission slip from his ruler to travel within his own country.

In the United States, passports were not only issued by the U.S. Department of State, but also by state governments, municipalities, and even notaries public. Issuances of these passports were quite rare and not required for traveling abroad. Craig Robertson of *Smithsonian Magazine* wrote, "[Passports] were more often used to gain access to private museums, collect mail from a post office, get invitations to social events, or to serve as a souvenir worth framing."[141] It wasn't until 1856 that Congress gave sole passport issuance authority to the Department of State, and required the person be a citizen. Despite this, however, there were still no requirements for having one to travel abroad or enter the U.S.

Prior to the end of World War I (1914–1918), the only requirements for traveling with a passport were temporary measures during the Revolutionary War (1775–1783) and the Civil War (1861–1865). On May 22, 1918, Congress passed the first law allowing the president to mandate a passport requirement during wartime.[142] Though the First World War ended six months later, the passport requirement remained in effect until President Woodrow Wilson left office on March 3, 1921.[143] The requirements were again reinstituted on June 21, 1941,[144]

---

141 Robertson, Craig. (February 7, 2017). "How the Passport Became an Improbable Symbol of American Identity". *Smithsonian Magazine*.

142 *An Act To prevent in time of war departure from or entry into the United States contrary to the public safety*. (May 22, 1918). 40 Stat. 559. Retrieved from https://govtrackus.s3.amazonaws.com/legislink/pdf/stat/40/STATUTE-40-Pg559.pdf

143 *Joint Resolution Declaring that certain Acts of Congress, joint resolutions, and proclamations shall be construed as if the war had ended and present or existing emergency expired*. (March 3, 1921). 41 Stat. 1359. Retrieved from https://govtrackus.s3.amazonaws.com/legislink/pdf/stat/41/STATUTE-41-Pg1359.pdf

144 *An Act To amend the Act of May 22, 1918 (40 Stat. 559)*. (June 21, 1941). 55 Stat.

and though they were intended to be temporary, not only were they never revoked, but they were officially made permanent by Congress on October 7, 1978.[145]

It would certainly be labeled tyranny if internal passports were required for a citizen to travel from Tennessee to Kentucky, and no one would make the proclamation that neither are a state because they do not control travel. Travel is a natural right, and any limits placed on that is tyranny. We have the natural right to travel, regardless if it is across the street, across the country, or across the world, and the fear that has been instilled in many people is irrational and unfounded. We are not subjects of His Majesty. Liberty is dangerous, but faith in the state is more so. Any reliance on government to protect us from the evils of the world is reliance on the illusion of security.

A talking point often repeated by conservatives is that anyone who supports open borders should remove the locks from their front doors and remove any fences they have around their property. This is a false equivalency. Private property is the tangible representation of one's labor. In nature, he was the one who labored in the land to grow the crops. In modern society, he was the one who exchanged his labor for the capital to purchase the home. This is what makes private property sovereign to its owner and gives him the right to defend it against trespassers.

The land of a nation, however, is not the same. While conquest has determined the borders and jurisdiction of the state, a government cannot own property. A government cannot labor, as its entire existence relies on stealing the property of its people in the form of taxation to sustain itself. What is commonly referred to as "public property" is simply land taken out from nature's state and gentrified using stolen property. It does not belong to the people unless the entire population consents to it. To say that it belongs to the collective is a socialist notion for this very

252. Retrieved from https://govtrackus.s3.amazonaws.com/legislink/pdf/stat/55/STATUTE-55-Pg252a.pdf

145 *Foreign Relations Authorization Act, Fiscal Year 1979*. (October 7, 1978). Pub.L. 95-426. Retrieved from https://www.govinfo.gov/content/pkg/STATUTE-92/pdf/STATUTE-92-Pg963.pdf

reason. It rightfully belongs to nature and therefore cannot be trespassed upon. No one would suggest it would be okay for only some people to utilize a "public" park while prohibiting others. Traveling on land to which another individual cannot rightfully claim as his is no different than wandering through an unexplored wilderness, even if surrounded by skyscrapers. No one can trespass on land unclaimed, and though we designate everything within the borders of the United States to be "our country," this cannot imply that we collectively own the nation as one owns property. A person immigrating into the United States, therefore, cannot trespass on nature's property. His mere presence in "our" country violates no one's rights, but our restriction of his entry will violate his.

The United States would still exist if the borders were opened to everyone. Of course, this cannot happen while the welfare state exists, but once abolished, open immigration would be a great benefit to our country. In his 1693 essay *For a General Naturalisation*, John Locke wrote:

> "...You need not fear, they will not remove hither to be in a worse state here. You may therefore safely open your doors, and a freedom to them to settle here being secure of this advantage that you have the profit of all their labour, for by that they pay for what they eat and spend of yours, unless you think it should be given to them for nothing which is not much to be feared."[146]

Simply put, immigrants come here to a new nation to better their lives. In doing so, they will stimulate economic growth, which is a huge benefit to all of us. We should welcome immigrants and treat them as our own. What would this mean for citizenship though? To that I ask the question, what exactly does it mean to be a citizen? In today's America, there is very little difference (for the average person) between a citizen and a non-citizen. There should not exist any class separation between the two, however, there does. Both citizens and non-citizens alike should have their natural rights fully recognized, however, there seems to be this notion, particularly among conservatives, that non-citizens should not have the right to bear arms, etc. The

---

146 Locke, John. (1693). *For a General Naturalisation.*

only real differences that exist between a citizen and a non-citizen is that a citizen has been granted the privilege of voting for elected officials and running for elected office.

The idea of birthright citizenship has been practiced throughout the centuries in various nations. In the United States, it was enshrined in the constitution with the simple clause outlining the qualifications to be eligible for the office of president. The question should be asked, however, as to what makes a natural-born citizen any more loyal to the ideals of a nation, than those of a naturalized citizen. It can easily be argued that a natural-born citizen takes his status for granted, whereas a naturalized citizen has far more of an appreciation for what it represents. As evidence of this, one will find that most naturalized citizens are far more outspoken against the ideas of socialism and communism, whereas many natural-born citizens advocate for their implementation.

A society that has only known plenty invariably will advocate for its redistribution. There is an adage that illustrates this point perfectly. Good times create weak men. Weak men create hard times. Hard times create strong men. Strong men create good times. This cycle exists because most governments are socialist in their very nature, and the expansion of government means the expansion of socialism. The easiest way to expand government is through the idea of universal suffrage rights. By extending the franchise to the entire citizenry, the overwhelming majority of which are always low-to-middle income earners, the citizenry is motivated to vote for candidates that promise to lift them from their current station in life. This engrains in them the notion that the path to a better life is through a simple stop at the ballot box. This is how socialism has always come into power. Frederick Engels, Karl Marx's right hand man, reiterated this point in his 1895 work, *The Revolutionary Act* (published in 1922). Engels says, "The Communist Manifesto had already proclaimed the struggle for the general franchise, for democracy, as one of the first and most important tasks of the militant proletariat."[147] To put it another way,

---

147 Engels, Frederick. (1895). "The Revolutionary Act: Military Insurrection Or Political and Economic Action?"

the will of "We the People" (aka the collective) is detrimental to the liberty of the individual.

Every individual should be free to choose for themselves where they live and how they handle their business without a state imposing arbitrary burdens at the will of the people. Just as a lie does not become truth simply because everyone believes it, tyranny is still tyranny even if everyone supports it. The will of the people is just as much of a threat to liberty as the state is. Only the individual has the right to make determinations for himself.

Chapter 9

Foreign Interventions

"The war is not meant to be won, it is meant to be continuous... The war is waged by the ruling group against its own subjects and its object is not the victory over either Eurasia or East Asia, but to keep the very structure of society intact." – George Orwell, 1984

I have heard it numerous times since I joined the military in 2005: "Thank you for serving our country." At first, it was humbling because I was proud of what I believed I was doing. I believed I was fighting to protect our liberty, but as this book has hopefully illustrated up to this point, liberty is on the brink of death. As I got older, as I buried friends, as I watched others struggle with mental scars, I began to question just for what exactly we were fighting. What was the real reason my friends were suffering? I was incredibly lucky during my time in the military. I never saw combat despite being deployed multiple times to combat zones. I know plenty of my fellow service members that were not so lucky, and I began to struggle myself over witnessing what they were going through.

Americans take pride in our military, and due to the terrible treatment of our troops returning from Vietnam, they go out of their way to show how much they support the troops. I need to be very clear when I say this: Americans genuinely support the men and women of the military, but they do so based on a lie they've been forced into believing. Speaking only for myself, I am proud of that chapter in my life, but I am not proud of my service. I did not do what everyone believes the military does. No one in the military does. We do not protect our liberty when we go off to war and have not done so since 1945.

Since the 1950s, the military has been reduced to nothing more than a political force made to serve the elites in power. Though many will look at the events of September 11, 2001 as an unprovoked attack on our liberty by radical Muslim terrorists, the truth is far more complex. The propaganda machines led the American public into believing that we were senselessly victimized on that day because Muslim terrorists hate our way of life. While I am in no way suggesting that the attack was justified, acceptable, or warranted, the hatred that groups like al-Qaeda have for the United States is not without merit. It runs far deeper than a simple religious war against those who do not convert to Islam. It was almost entirely due to United States foreign policy dating back decades.

To fully understand why groups like al-Qaeda despise the United States, we must go back to the 1930s. Following the Great Depression, disagreements between the Iranian government and the British-owned Anglo-Persian Oil Company (APOC, which operated within Iranian borders) led to renegotiations of the original contract set a decade earlier. In 1933, a new agreement was reached which mandated that APOC reduce its area of control to 100,000 square-miles, ensured that royalty payments made to the Iranian government would not fall below £4 million, and stated "a promise that more Iranians would be trained for administrative positions."[148] As part of the agreement, APOC changed its name to Anglo-Iranian Oil Company (AIOC), which helped give Iranians a greater sense of ownership over the British company than it actually had.

Over the next decade and a half, AIOC continuously failed to live up to its 1933 agreement. In 1950, the Arabian-American Oil Company (known as Aramco, which at the time was a conglomerate of Standard Oil of California, Standard Oil of New York, Standard Oil of New Jersey, and Texaco, and would later become Saudi Aramco) reached a deal with Saudi Arabia in which profits were split 50/50 between the Saudi government and the Aramco partners. Iran sought a similar deal with AIOC, but the British government outright refused. Less than 6 months later, the Iranian Parliament (known as the Majlis) unanimously voted to fully nationalize AIOC, and elected Mohammad Mossadegh as its Prime Minister, granting him emergency powers superior to those of

---

148 Kinzer, Stephen (2003). "All the Shah's Men: An American Coup and the Roots of Middle East Terror". *John Wiley & Sons.*

the Iranian King (known as the Shah).[149] Mossadegh was a fierce voice against British control over Iran's oil and began rallying the support of the people.

British Prime Minister Winston Churchill began talks with President Harry Truman in 1951 regarding assistance in the crisis in which they now found themselves. President Truman was deeply invested in armed resistance in Korea, but also sided with Mossadegh's views. Stephen Kinzer wrote in his 2003 book, *All the Shah's Men* that "[Truman] had nothing but contempt for old-style imperialists like those who ran Anglo-Iranian. Besides, the CIA had never overthrown a government, and Truman did not wish to set the precedent."[150] In 1953, however, Truman left office, and Eisenhower took his place. Eisenhower was far more along the philosophical lines of Churchill and wasted no time in implementing CIA intervention, especially when Churchill put a Cold War spin on his issue.

There were two problems they sought to overcome: first, they needed to remove Mossadegh from power and reinstitute the current Shah (who was sympathetic to Britain's goal) with his full power, and second, the communist Tudeh Party, though not a full backer of Mossadegh, was gaining power in Iran and shared Mossadegh's goal of eliminating the Iranian monarchy entirely. Mossadegh's influence and powers amassed from Parliament caused the current Shah, Mohammad Reza Pahlavi (also known as Mohammad Reza Shah), to flee Iran on February 26, 1953.

In declassified documents, CIA Director Allen Dulles (brother of Eisenhower's secretary of state and former senator from New York, John Foster Dulles), sent a memo to President Eisenhower on March 1, 1953, a mere 40 days after taking office, explaining the situation:

> *"Ever since the… diplomatic break with Britain over the oil negotiations, the Iranian situation has been slowly disintegrating. The result has been a steady decrease in the power and influence of the Western*

---

149 NOTE: Documents cited will spell Mohammad Mossadegh's name in several ways, including Mossadeq, Mosadeq, and Mosaddegh. All quotes used will reflect the spelling used in the original document.
150 Kinzer (2003).

democracies and the building up of a situation where a Communist takeover is becoming more and more of a possibility. However, even the present crisis is likely to be unsatisfactorily compromised without a Communist Tudeh victory. Of course, the elimination of Mossadeq by assassination or otherwise might precipitate decisive events except in the unlikely alternative that the Shah should regain courage and decisiveness...

"Retired General Zahedi, currently imprisoned by Mossadeq, also wishes to become Prime Minister, and his adherents are active in the Majlis. It is unlikely that he will succeed. The present situation offers the Shah an opportunity which he has not as yet seized. His past record does not suggest that he will act."[151]

Operation Ajax was officially launched, and the CIA orchestrated its first covert coup d'état to overthrow a foreign government.[152] Two days following the March 1 memo to Eisenhower, the CIA released another memo outlining their clandestine capabilities to institute a coup d'état. These included the following:

- Mass propaganda
- Poison pen, personal denunciations, rumor spreading, etc.
- Street riots, demonstrations, mobs, etc.
- Tribal support
- Assisting Iranians at internal security
- One additional means not declassified[153]

Over the next several months, the CIA would carry out these capabilities in Iran. Kermit Roosevelt, Jr., grandson of former President Theodore Roosevelt, was the lead CIA agent overseeing the operation

---

151 Dulles, Allen. (March 1, 1953). "Memorandum From Director of Central Intelligence Dulles to President Eisenhower". Retrieved from https://static.history.state.gov/frus/frus1951-54Iran/pdf/frus1951-54Iran.pdf
152 Gasiorowski, Mark J. (August 19,1998). "The 1953 Coup D'état in Iran". Retrieved from http://iran.sa.utoronto.ca/coup/web_files/markcoup.html
153 Unknown. (March 3, 1953). "Memorandum Prepared in the Directorate of Plans, Central Intelligence Agency". Retrieved from https://static.history.state.gov/frus/frus1951-54Iran/pdf/frus1951-54Iran.pdf

on the ground in Tehran, using the U.S. Embassy as his base of operations. U.S. Ambassador, Loy W. Henderson, was obviously well aware of this fact, but served to ensure Mossadegh remained in the dark about the operation. Several attempts to arrest Mossadegh had failed in early August, and on the evening of August 18, he met with Ambassador Henderson. The same declassified documents say that Henderson "was inclined to believe that Mossedeq was suspicious that the United States Government or at least United States officials were either implicated in the effort to oust him or were sympathetically aware of such an effort in advance."[154]

The next day, Prime Minister Mossadegh was successfully arrested by Iranians on the CIA payroll. The media (per CIA directives) reported that Mossadegh had been killed, and that his standing orders appointed General Fazlollah Zahedi to be his successor. With Zahedi in place, Mohammad Reza Shah was able to return to Iran. In 1954, a new agreement was reached that created a consortium of oil producers to operate in Iran under the umbrella holding corporation known as Iranian Oil Participants, Ltd (IOP). The Consortium Agreement renamed the Anglo-Iranian Oil Company to British Petroleum (BP) and split the holdings as follows:

- British Petroleum – 40%
- Royal Dutch Shell – 14%
- Gulf Oil (later Chevron) – 8%
- Aramco partner Standard Oil of California (later Chevron) – 8%
- Aramco partner Standard Oil of New Jersey (later Exxon, then ExxonMobil) – 8%
- Aramco partner Standard Oil of New York (later Mobil, then ExxonMobil) – 8%
- Aramco partner Texaco (later Chevron) – 8%
- French Petroleum Company (later TotalEnergies) – 6%[155]

---

154 Unknown. (August 19, 1953). "Memorandum for the Record". Retrieved from https://static.history.state.gov/frus/frus1951-54Iran/pdf/frus1951-54Iran.pdf
155 Vassilliou, Marius S. (2009). "Historical Dictionary of the Petroleum Industry: Volume 3". *Scarecrow Press*.

Once the Shah regained his power, the Iranian people needed to be kept in check since Mossadegh was revered by them even after the coup d'état. In 1957, with the assistance of the CIA and Israeli intelligence officers, the Shah created a gestapo-like police force known as the SAVAK (an acronym that translates to Organization for National Intelligence and Security) charged with the mission of sustaining the Iranian monarchy. Though officially a civilian organization, most of the 15,000 SAVAK officers were simultaneously serving in the Iranian armed forces.[156]

In 1963, the Shah launched what was known as the "White Revolution" which "called for land reform, nationalization of the forests, the sale of state-owned enterprises to private interests, electoral changes to enfranchise women, profit sharing in industry, and an anti-illiteracy campaign in the nation's schools."[157] It was the land reforms specifically that caused outrage among Iranians, and in particular, the Shi'ah ulama (religious scholars). The Iranian population was 90% Muslim, and most of the ulama were landowners that relied on rental income to fund their mosques.[158] One of these ulama was Ayatollah Ruhollah Khomeini, who viewed the Shah's revolution as one against Islam itself and became one of the Shah's most outspoken critics.

On June 5, 1963, the SAVAK arrested Khomeini and imprisoned him for ten months, during which he never backed down from his criticisms. The Shah exiled him to Turkey and later to Iraq. Despite his exile, Khomeini continued to criticize the Shah's totalitarianism as well as the United States for ensuring his return to power a decade earlier. He made cassette tapes that slowly made their way back to Iran, which incited anti-Shah demonstrations. The Shah instituted martial law, and the SAVAK invoked their wrath on anyone who disobeyed. This caused much civil unrest and crippled the Iranian economy.[159]

---

156 Library of Congress. (2008). "Iran: A Country Study". Retrieved from https://web.archive.org/web/20171010060505/http://www.loc.gov/rr/frd/cs/pdf/CS_Iran.pdf
157 Thorton, Ted. (2007). "The Arab-Israeli Wars: 1948–1973". Retrieved from https://web.archive.org/web/20071224172550/http://www.nmhschool.org/tthornton/mehistorydatabase/arabisraeliwars.htm#white%20revolution
158 Mackey, Sandra (1996). "The Iranians: Persia, Islam, and the Soul of a Nation".
159 Vengencefrom1979 (November 26, 2010). "A Brief History of Iran – 1953 to Present". Retrieved from https://www.youtube.com/watch?v=jPcFfesAzBw

In 1978, President Jimmy Carter sent General Robert Huyser, the Deputy Commander of NATO, into Iran to "facilitate contact" between the Shah and Khomeini's followers in Tehran, but this effort failed.[160] The Iranians believed that once again the Americans were attempting to overthrow their revolution and keep Mohammad Reza Shah in power. On January 16, 1979, Khomeini's followers forced the Shah to flee Iran once again, as he had done in 1953. That same day, the United States froze the Shah's assets to prevent them from being seized by Iranian revolutionaries. For the first time since his exile, Ruhollah Khomeini returned to Iran and was named Supreme Leader on February 11. On October 22, Mohammad Reza Shah was admitted to the United States to undergo medical treatment for gallstones. Three weeks later, an organization loyal to Khomeini known as the Muslim Student Followers of the Imam's Line, stormed the U.S. Embassy in Tehran, the very same embassy from which the CIA carried out the 1953 coup d'état. This incident is now known as the Iranian Hostage Crisis. The students had four demands:

1. Return Mohammad Reza Shah to Iran to stand trial
2. Return the Iranian assets frozen by the United States (much of which were profits from Iranian oil sales)
3. Apologize for the United States' role in Iranian affairs, including the overthrow of Prime Minister Mohammad Mossadegh
4. Promise that the United States will never again interfere in Iranian affairs

On January 19, 1981, the day before Ronald Reagan would be sworn in as president, President Carter signed the Algiers Accords, which was a negotiated agreement between the students and the United States. In it, the U.S. agreed to unfreeze the Iranian assets and promised to never interfere in Iranian affairs, but would not turn Mohammad Reza Pahlavi over to Iran nor acknowledge their prior involvements (though

---

160 Mílaní, Abbas. (May 22, 2012). "The Shah". *St. Martin's Publishing Group.*

the trove of now-declassified documents proves it to be so). Ruhollah Khomeini was officially recognized as the Iranian Supreme Leader as a result. The following day, the students released the hostages, ending the 444 day siege.

Around the same time that the hostage crisis began, unrest was growing in Afghanistan. Following the Saur Revolution in 1978, the Afghan government was now under control of the Soviet-backed People's Democratic Party of Afghanistan (PDPA). The preceding 5 years had seen steady armed conflict after the 1973 Soviet-backed coup d'état overthrew Mohammad Zahir Shah. Devout Sunni Muslims saw the secular communist government as an abomination to Islam and began to revolt. Eventually, these revolts led to the Soviet Union committing troops to Afghanistan to help fight the rebel cells, marking the beginning of the Soviet-Afghan War.

All of these events and their histories were known around the Muslim world, and in particular, they were known by a 22-year-old civil engineering student at King Abdulaziz University in Jeddah, Saudi Arabia, named Usama bin Laden. It was there that he studied under professor and fellow Muslim Brotherhood member Abdullah Azzam. In 1984, Azzam and bin Laden founded an organization called Maktab al-Khidamat (MAK) in order to help acquire money, weapons, and personnel to fight with the mujahedeen against the Soviets and reclaim Afghanistan for the Sunnis.

Of course, the U.S. government felt the need to inject itself into the conflict in order to stop the spread of communism, but also due to the assassination of U.S. Ambassador to Afghanistan Adolph Dubs. In what was dubbed by the CIA as Operation Cyclone, the U.S. government, in partnership with the British MI6 and Pakistani Inter-Service Intelligence (ISI), began funneling weapons to multiple mujahedeen cells, including MAK. Politically spearheaded by Texas Congressman Charlie Wilson, an unofficial deal was cut with the Saudi Arabian government where they would match all funding from the CIA dollar-for-dollar.[161]

In 1988, bin Laden, along with Azzam and Ayman al-Zawahiri,

---

161 Crile, George (2003). "Charlie Wilson's War: The Extraordinary Story of the Longest Covert Operation in History". *The Atlantic Press*.

split from MAK and founded al-Qaeda. This shifted their roles from support and training administrators to frontline combatants. The following year, the Soviets withdrew from Afghanistan, and bin Laden returned to Saudi Arabia as a hero.[162] On August 2, 1990, Iraqi President Saddam Hussein launched a full-scale invasion into Kuwait. Outraged by this threat to Saudi Arabia, bin Laden approached Saudi Defense Minister, Prince Sultan bin Abdelazziz al-Saud and urged him to reject American assistance. Bin Laden viewed the act of nonbelievers entering the kingdom to be insulting, as Saudi Arabia is home to the holiest city in Islam, Mecca. Despite offering 100,000 al-Qaeda soldiers who were former mujahedeen, Prince Sultan rejected bin Laden. Five days later, the first 15,000 American troops arrived in Saudi Arabia, along with 32 navy destroyers, and 100 fighter jets and attack helicopters, marking the beginning of Operation Desert Storm. Feeling betrayed by his people, bin Laden began fiercely criticizing the Saudi government. In 1992, bin Laden called for its overthrow, and in 1994, they stripped bin Laden of his citizenship, and he fled the country for Sudan and later returned to Afghanistan.[163]

In 1996, despite previously fighting for the mujahedeen during the Soviet-Afghan War, and training at the camps run by Azzam, a wealthy Pakistani engineer named Khalid Sheikh Mohammad first met bin Laden at Tora Bora in Afghanistan. During this meeting, the idea that would become the 9/11 attacks on the World Trade Center was first plotted. The question as to why the U.S. was targeted is no longer a difficult question to answer, given the history of America's involvement in the region spanning several decades. In fact, bin Laden himself answered it in a video addressed to the American people in 2004:

"Before I begin, I say to you that security is an indispensable pillar of human life and that free men do not forfeit their security, contrary to Bush's claim that we hate freedom. If so, then let him explain to us why we don't

---

162 "Who is bin Laden? Chronology". (2010). Retrieved from https://web.archive.org/web/20100414023118/http://www.pbs.org/wgbh/pages/frontline/shows/binladen/etc/cron.html

163 Jehl, Douglas. (December 27, 2001). "A Nation Challenged; Saudi Arabia; Holy War Lured Saudis as Rulers Looked Away". *New York Times*.

*strike for example – Sweden... No, we fight because we are free men who
don't sleep under oppression. We want to restore freedom to our nation,
just as you lay waste to our nation, so shall we lay waste to yours...*

*The events that affected my soul in a direct way started in
1982 when America permitted the Israelis to invade Lebanon and
the American Sixth Fleet helped them in that. This bombardment began and many were killed and injured and others were terrorized
and displaced. I couldn't forget those moving scenes, blood and severed
limbs, women and children sprawled everywhere. Houses destroyed
along with their occupants and high rises demolished over their residents, rockets raining down on our home without mercy. The situation was like a crocodile meeting a helpless child, powerless except for
his screams. Does the crocodile understand a conversation that doesn't
include a weapon? And the whole world saw and heard but it didn't
respond.*

*In those difficult moments many hard-to-describe ideas bubbled
in my soul, but in the end they produced an intense feeling of rejection
of tyranny, and gave birth to a strong resolve to punish the oppressors.
And as I looked at those demolished towers in Lebanon, it entered my
mind that we should punish the oppressor in kind and that we should
destroy towers in America in order that they taste some of what we
tasted and so that they be deterred from killing our women and children. And that day, it was confirmed to me that oppression and the intentional killing of innocent women and children is a deliberate American policy. Destruction is freedom and democracy, while resistance is
terrorism and intolerance.*

*This means the oppressing and embargoing to death of millions
as Bush, Sr. did in Iraq in the greatest mass slaughter of children mankind has ever known, and it means the throwing of millions of pounds
of bombs and explosives at millions of children – also in Iraq – as Bush,
Jr. did, in order to remove an old agent and replace him with a new
puppet to assist in the pilfering of Iraq's oil and other outrages... So I
say to you, over 15,000 of our people have been killed and tens of thousands injured, while more than a thousand of you have been killed and
more than 10,000 injured. And Bush's hands are stained with the blood*

138

Foreign Interventions

of all those killed from both sides, all for the sake of oil and keeping their private companies in business...[164]

America's involvement in foreign nations has been rampant and unchecked for decades. These interventions are written off by the American public using the vague euphemism of "American interests overseas." Aside from the direct involvement on the ground, sanctions levied by the U.S. have also caused incredible amounts of destruction in the region with zero concern from members of the government. In 1996, *60 Minutes* correspondent Lesley Stahl asked then-U.N. Ambassador Madeleine Albright if the sanctions on Iraq had been worth the 500,000 children that had died as a result. Her answer, without hesitation, was "I think that is a very hard choice, but the price, we think, the price is worth it."[165]

Following the 2016 presidential election, accusations came out suggesting that the Russian government had interfered in the election process in order to ensure a win for Donald Trump. Though no direct link was found between Russian operatives and the Trump campaign, the very notion that a foreign nation had interfered in the election process rightfully angered many Americans, especially after the Mueller report found that "the Russian government interfered in the 2016 presidential election in sweeping and systematic fashion."[166] Now, imagine for a moment that instead of simple election interference, the Russian government orchestrated a coup d'état to overthrow an incredibly popular president, such as Ronald Reagan for example, and install a pro-Russian tyrant in his place. Imagine Russian oil corporations drilling oil on U.S. soil, exporting it to Russia, and compensating the U.S. pennies of the proceeds to do so. Imagine the Russian government instituting sanctions on the U.S. that resulted in nearly 8 million American children

---

164 Bin Laden, Usama (November 1, 2004). "Full Transcript of bin Ladin's Speech". *Al Jazeera*. Retrieved from https://web.archive.org/web/20081116092323/http://english. aljazeera.net/archive/2004/11/200849163336457223.html
165 CBS News. (May 12, 1996). "Punishing Saddam". Retrieved from https://www. youtube.com/watch?v=bntsfiAXMEE
166 Mueller, Robert S. III. (March 2019). "Report on the Investigation into Russian Interference in the 2016 Presidential Election".

dying as a result (keeping the proportions the same to the Iraqi population in 1996). At what point would you decide to declare war on the Russian government?

The U.S. government's intervention in foreign nations has had massive effects on the state of liberty. The propaganda machine has done everything in its power to ensure that the state is made to be the victim and that good citizens are needed to serve its interests. The reality, however, is that these brave men and women that selflessly sign up to serve their country only end up serving the interests of the political elites. Many of them come home in flag-draped coffins, while others come back with a lifetime of mental scars. Defending American liberty has not been an actual mission of the U.S. armed services for the better part of a century, if not longer. This act of defrauding of every single individual who signs up to serve the state is an act of pure evil. Not only does it violate the rights of other peoples abroad, but the con by which the state sways young, ambitious minds, is at the very least ethically bankrupt.

Part II:
The Solution to the State

Chapter 10

What is Liberty Not?

"A man is no less a slave because he is allowed to choose a new master once in a term of years." – Lysander Spooner

In Part I, I laid out a very simplistic foundation as to what liberty is. This is being revisited here in Part II for two reasons. First, a case against the state has yet to be made. It was necessary to define liberty in order to prove the grievances thereafter, but the solution needed to remain somewhat ambiguous; and this segues into the second reason. While you may have read and even agreed with the words I used to define liberty in the first chapter, there is a likelihood that the full appreciation of the definition was not realized. This is not some condescending statement designed to belittle. It is actually just a function of the human psyche. Human psychology tends to fill one's own unconscious biases into any gaps that may exist in one's philosophy if it has not been fully explored by the individual, and this is where a large part of intellectual inconsistencies are created.

Many people, despite claiming their desires for liberty, are actually statist in their overall philosophies. This would include those who believe in a state solely for the defense of liberty (the minarchist), as well as the constitutional conservative who believes in a modernized vision of America's Founding Fathers. When I started writing this book, I identified as a minarchist. As my research into this treatise went on, I realized that the problem with statism, regardless of how small one wishes it to be, is simple. As the adage goes, "Power corrupts. Absolute power corrupts absolutely."

Any state, no matter how small, will invariably grow more powerful and more corrupt, regardless of what constitutional limits are established. As a perfect illustration of this fact, the U.S. Constitution is quite clear in many of its limits set upon the federal government. Despite this, however, they have grown far beyond their constitutional limitations. The oldest example of such disregard for constitutional limitation that I can find dates to the *Marbury v. Madison* ruling in 1803. Despite Article III of the constitution not specifically granting the Supreme Court the power of judicial review and the 10th Amendment explicitly stating that powers not delegated by the constitution are reserved for the states, the notion of so-called "implied powers" was born. Since then, the unchecked power of the Supreme Court to determine the constitutionality of law has been the mechanism by which the federal government has been allowed to surpass its limits.

The problems with Supreme Court rulings has been highlighted in Part I, and to the constitutional conservative, the solution would be to implement more checks on the Supreme Court, but those checks require the involvement of the same organization that is issuing the usurping rulings: the government. Some might suggest, as former Vice President John C. Calhoun did, that the state governments have some sort of check over the federal Supreme Court, but this poses its own problem. Murray N. Rothbard, philosopher and cofounder of both the CATO Institute and the Ludwig von Mises Institute, put it this way in his 1974 book, *Anatomy of the State*:

> *"If any substantial minority interest in the country, specifically a state government, believed that the Federal Government was exceeding its powers and encroaching on that minority, the minority would have the right to veto this exercise of power as unconstitutional. Applied to state governments, this theory implied the right of 'nullification' of a Federal law or ruling within a state's jurisdiction. In theory, the ensuing constitutional system would assure that the Federal Government check any state invasion of individual rights, while the states would check excessive Federal power over the individual. And yet, while limitations would undoubtedly be more effective than at present, there are many difficulties and problems in the Calhoun solution. If, indeed, a subordinate interest should rightfully have a veto over matters concerning it, then why stop with the states? Why not place veto power in counties,*

cities, wards? Furthermore, interests are not only sectional, they are also occupational, social, etc. What of bakers or taxi drivers or any other occupation? Should they not be permitted a veto power over their own lives? This brings us to the important point that the nullification theory confines its checks to agencies of government itself. Let us not forget that federal and state governments, and their respective branches, are still states, are still guided by their own state interests rather than by the interests of the private citizens."[167]

From this analysis, we can see that the state still plays the role of arbiter on behalf of all people within their jurisdiction. This role still allows the state to have a greater say over the lives and property of all individuals than the individual has. This, by its very definition, is tyranny.

For the statist, any check they place on the state, as Rothbard said, must be executed by the state itself. Try as individuals might to have a state that exists solely to protect liberty, tyranny will always be the product of the state. Liberty, therefore, is *not* found in statism. To help illustrate this, consider an analogy where liberty is personified as an individual. To this individual, statism would be cancer, the various stages of which would be reflective of how tyrannical the state would be. What minimal statists suggest per their philosophies would be no different than an oncologist telling an individual that the key to protecting one's health is a minimal amount of cancer. Of course, this is completely untrue.

Let us consider the minarchist state for a moment and test the theory that it preserves liberty as I once believed. The constitution of such a state would be incredibly simple and leave no room for interpretation. It would require the state to have very specific legislative powers pertaining only to matters of murder, rape, assault, and the like, an agency to enforce those laws, a court system to charge and prosecute those laws, and possibly a prison system for punitive purposes. The first question to arise is how the various state employees and projects get funded. Immediately, liberty is destroyed, as the minarchist state requires the usurpation of property rights in the form of taxation. I have heard it proposed by other

---

167 Rothbard, Murray N. (1974). "Anatomy of the State". *Ludwig von Mises Institute.*

minarchists that all taxation be voluntarily paid, which would absolve the state of this usurpation, but this creates its own problems.

Assume the minarchist state functions with nearly all of its people voluntarily contributing their tax offerings save for one. Bill has decided against volunteering to offer his property to the state. When his friend Jeff confronts him about it, an argument breaks out where Jeff assaults Bill to a degree in which Bill decides to press assault charges. At this point, Bill is utilizing services provided by the state without ever volunteering his property in order to help fund them. In effect, Bill is stealing from the state and is therefore stealing from the population. After all, using a product or service without first paying for it is theft. If taxation is voluntary, then no enforcement mechanisms exist to prevent this form of theft.

This also highlights another usurpation of liberty: arrest. Arrest is no different than kidnapping, and should anyone who is not an agent of the state do it or attempt to do it to another, even in today's society, it would be charged as such. Some legal exceptions do apply with citizen arrest laws, but at its basic foundation, arrest is still the act of holding someone against their will. This sentiment is especially true when one holds the supposed mantra of "innocent until proven guilty" in the highest regard. If the individual is supposed to be treated as if they are innocent, why are they taken against their will in chains and held in a cage until trial concludes months, or even years later? Innocent people are not treated this way, but guilty people should not be either.

There is a notion that is held by nearly all people, including Rothbard, that an individual somehow gives up or surrenders their rights when they aggress against another individual. Though this statement will be wildly unpopular, the notion of giving up one's rights must be declared invalid in its entirety. Rights cannot be given up or surrendered, as that is what differentiates them from privileges. If rights are to be viewed as capable of being surrendered, suspended, or revoked, then they are not rights at all but merely privileges contingent upon a criteria established by others.

Liberty cannot exist so long as one individual has more of a say over the life and property of another. If any exception is made to this rule whatsoever, then tyranny exists. Going back to my previous analogy about cancer, a person either has cancer or they do not. The same holds true for tyranny; it either exists or it does not. Any amount of tyranny, no matter how small, removes liberty from existence. The only way for liberty to exist is in the absence of the state. In short, liberty only exists in the state of anarchy. While the idea of anarchy has been skewed by many who mistakenly believe it to be a state of chaos and disorder, a stateless or anarchist society would necessarily be its polar opposite, and this will be expounded on throughout Part II.

There are multiple philosophies regarding anarchy; the two most popular of which are anarcho-communism and anarcho-capitalism. Anarcho-communism is the philosophy in which a stateless society exists, private property does not, and goods are redistributed using the Marxist mantra of "from each according to his ability, to each according to his needs." Anarcho-capitalism, on the other hand, is the philosophy that promotes a stateless society where private property and the voluntary exchange thereof is paramount. One point in particular that statists like to highlight as a means of opposing any anarchist system is lack of historical precedent. Anarcho-communists and anarcho-capitalists alike have laid claims of such societies existing, but admittedly, the point is not entirely moot. Anarcho-communists, for example, like to tell of the society created by Kim Chwa-chin in Korea in 1929. This society was home to over two million Koreans, and according to the anarcho-communist, was entirely devoid of the state while community needs were met through voluntary sharing of goods. While this was close to a stateless society, it was not truly so. Modern day anarcho-communist philosopher, Peter Gelderloos, wrote in 2010 the following describing it:

> *"Using assemblies and a decentralized federative structure that grew out of the [Korean Anarchist Communist Federation], they created village councils, district councils, and area councils to deal with matters of cooperative agriculture, education, and finance.... Caught between the Stalinists and the Japanese imperial army, the autonomous province was ultimately crushed in 1931. But for two years, large populations*

had freed themselves from the authority of landlords and governors and reasserted their power to come to collective decisions, to organize their day-to-day life, pursue their dreams, and defend those dreams from invading armies."[168]

This structure that Gelderloos describes is the very anatomy that comprises a state, particularly in the form of the councils. Councils by their very nature are authoritarian, meaning decisions would be made and subsequently enforced in order to keep the society functioning. This was more of a minarchist society than anything and despite it reportedly existing without private property ownership and operating without any form of currency, "the staff of the departments received no more than the average wage."[169]

There is one major issue, however, with the Korean example, as well as with anarcho-communism generally. As Marx wrote, and as was previously highlighted in Part I, the abolition of private property is required for a communist society to exist. If private property is to not be recognized as a natural right, then the aggressive acts of theft and trespassing cannot therefore be recognized as acts of aggression. If Bill goes out into the wilderness, fells timber, and constructs a home with his bare hands, then the anarcho-communist philosophy dictates that home belongs to everyone should they wish to use it. Despite Bill being the sole laborer in its construction, the fruits of his labor would be shared by everyone. He could not even lay claim to the master bedroom as his, and should he find it occupied by a stranger, he has no right to demand the stranger leave. Moreover, should he also have solely tilled the land and grew corn, he would also have no claim against anyone who takes possession of his stalks without his knowledge or permission.

The entire concept of communism requires central planning in all aspects to ensure its goals are achieved. Centralization of any kind requires an authoritarian enforcement mechanism to ensure compliance

---

168 Gelderloos, Peter (2010). "Anarchy Works". *The Anarchist Library*.
169 MacSimoin, Alan. (2005). "The Korean Anarchist Movement". *The Anarchist Library*.

by everyone involved. Standards must be established as to what constitutes a state of destitution (i.e. what minimum requirements must be set for housing, clothing, food, etc.). A means of mitigating the classes must also be established, as well as a means of handling noncompliance. These few key points ultimately make anarcho-communism to be a philosophy antithetical to itself.

The other major school of thought surrounding the anarchist philosophy is that of anarcho-capitalism, and this is where our solutions surrounding the current state of liberty begin.

Chapter 11

The Two Forms of Property

"Property is surely a right of mankind as real as liberty."
– John Adams

The view that property ownership is a natural right should not be up for debate, yet socialists and communists seem to lack the understanding of what makes it so. As previously discussed, an individual's labor is what grants him the right to claim ownership over it. This means that in an anarcho-capitalist society, property can only exist in two forms: natural (or unclaimed) property and private property. Natural property is simple to explain: it is the land as created by nature. The only other stipulation for natural property would be private property that has been abandoned. Of course a property owner has full right to abandon his property should he so choose, and once done, this effectively transfers title back to nature. Property completely devoid of maintenance by man deteriorates as nature begins to reclaim it. Structures begin to crumble, plants grow without prejudice, and fences and foundations become decrepit. These are the telltale signs that nature has reclaimed title over a piece of previously owned property.

The other form of property is private property. This is property that has been taken out of the state of nature and transformed according to the property owner's wishes. Private property may then be transferred to a new owner via gift, voluntary exchange, or abandonment (in which case the new owner becomes nature itself). As you will no doubt recall from Part I, the so-called "public property" is not a valid form of property due to the fact that it was created from property extorted from the people. The question must therefore be raised as to who would have ownership of these properties should the state be entirely dissolved.

Rothbard beautifully explained the foundational solution to a similar problem in his 1982 book, *The Ethics of Liberty*:

> *"[T]his is by no means a critical problem, for, as we have seen, where victims are lost to antiquity, the land properly belongs to any non-criminals who are in current possession. Suppose, for example, that Henry Jones I stole a piece of land from its legitimate owner, James Smith. What is the current status of the title of current possessor Henry Jones X? Or of the man who might be the current possessor by purchasing the land from Henry Jones X? If Smith and his descendants are lost to antiquity, then title to the land properly and legitimately belongs to the current Jones (or the man who has purchased it from him), in direct application of our theory of property titles."*[170]

In the case of "public property," the state extorted private property from the people in order to fund the development of that piece of land. Though Rothbard's "lost to antiquity" argument could be made, it would be simpler to describe this as lost to complexity. It is a virtual impossibility to not only identify each individual from whom the state extorted the property, but also to calculate how much equity each would have in that land. Since the state is a criminal possessor, and the complexity of calculating ownership is an impossible task, all "public property" must be rightfully considered to be natural property.

Does this mean all of the city parks, streets, highways, and state buildings are up for grabs by the first individual who claims it as his? Not exactly. Remember that it is an individual's labor that grants him the title of ownership over natural property. For Bill to claim ownership over all 2,460 miles of Interstate 10, for example (which runs from Santa Monica, CA to Jacksonville, FL), he must first introduce his labor onto the highway in order to transform it from its current state. Even then, he can only claim title of ownership over the portion on which he labored. Repainting the lanes on a quarter-mile stretch of highway does not grant him title over the entirety of I-10, just as planting a single tomato plant does not entitle the farmer to claim title over the entirety of a continent.

170 Rothbard, Murray N. (1982). "The Ethics of Liberty". *New York University Press*.

In reality, should the state be eradicated throughout the land currently making up the United States, numerous companies big and small would seek to claim the various roads and highways that are currently built. This would mean that everything from I-10 to the street connected to your driveway would be privately owned property. While at first, the sudden shock to the market would no doubt cause an incredible amount of volatility, the entire market would eventually stabilize, and a plethora of solutions would be tailored for market needs. It is this shock, however, on which most people tend to focus when presented with the idea of privatized roads, and they usually pair it with a wildly outlandish scenario, such as a toll collector being posted outside of everyone's driveway who would refuse to lift the gate blocking your vehicle until they are paid the fee. Though theoretically possible, the chances of this scenario actually playing out would be negligible. After all, since capitalism is the voluntary exchange of property for a good or service, it behooves the providers of those goods and services to ensure their business practices are aligned with the market itself. Assuming they had the startup capital to pay wages for a sufficient number of toll workers to man the booths stationed at each driveway (an unlikelihood in and of itself), such a business practice would surely cause their clientele to outright revolt against the company, likely violently.

It is highly likely that most residents in communities throughout the United States would not notice any difference in how their residential streets are managed should the state be abolished. This is because anywhere a homeowner association (HOA) exists, the residential streets are already privately owned and managed. The way subdivisions are developed are actually quite reflective of how an anarcho-capitalist society would work, though it does have its differences. To illustrate an example, imagine Winston Developers, Inc. purchases a 100-acre plot of land just outside of Anytown, USA. Before a single shovel breaks the soil, this land is rightfully the private property of Winston Developers, and they begin planning for the development of the neighborhood. They plan the layout of the streets, lot lines, and basic designs of the homes to be built and subsequently hire contractors to begin construction. When prospective buyers come to look at homes in the development, the sales agent informs them of the HOA monthly dues as a condition for purchase. Aside from maintenance of the private streets, these dues also cover other amenities the neighborhood has to offer, such as a community pool, gym, and parks. When the developer sells a home, they have predetermined the property lines for the sale, which excludes the streets. The streets, as well as the other amenity plots remain under Winston Development's private ownership until they transfer title to the HOA itself. This HOA is another private company created by the developer, whose board members are initially appointed by Winston Development. When the neighborhood nears completion, the Winston appointees begin to transfer their positions to residents who seek to hold them. When transfer is complete, the HOA is still a private company but is run by the residents themselves.

HOAs certainly sound similar to the councils created in Korea that I criticized in the last chapter, so what makes an HOA perfectly acceptable by comparison? The recognition of private property as a natural right is what makes all of the difference. In the Korean example, private property was not recognized as a natural right, and thus an arbitrary enforcement mechanism was required to ensure producers complied with distribution requirements. This by its very definition is a government. The HOA, on the other hand, is a private company created by Winston Developers, which already had rightful ownership over the entire plot of land before any homes were built. As property owner, Winston was able to set any terms they wished as a condition of sale. Think of these conditions as having no difference between the "End User Agreement" or "Terms of Use" that appear on your Facebook or Hulu accounts. If the buyer voluntarily agrees to those terms, then a contract is established between the two parties. Since property rights were not recognized in the Korean example, no voluntary contract was ever made between the farmer and the council. Whatever he produced was shared among the community following the "From each according to their ability, to each according to their need," mantra. This is what differentiates the Korean council's existence as a state entity and the HOA's existence as a private company.

Though problems do exist in some of today's HOAs, such as an overzealous HOA board attempting to fine a homeowner out of an arbitrary fee for their grass being too tall, these issues could safely be ignored in an anarcho-capitalist society. The authority of an HOA does extend past the property line that separates the individual's private property from that of the HOA. This point, however, raises the question surrounding deed restrictions. The owner of any property by natural right has sole dominion and sovereignty over his property, just as every individual has the same over his own life. While an HOA may adopt guidelines for the neighborhood to follow, any attempt to coerce a property owner into compliance would be a violation of his rights. The only means by which such stipulations would be valid would be if all properties in the neighborhood were actually owned by the HOA and the residents rented the homes. In this situation, the HOA would have title over the property itself, and thus would have the right to set any contractual stipulations for leasing any property.

Many might counter that deed restrictions are valid, as they are a condition of purchasing the property, and while this sounds reasonable on its face, it actually is not. Once the title for a piece of property is transferred to a new owner, it is impossible for the previous owner to continue to have any say in how that property is used. To illustrate this logic, let us assume that Roger sold his 1965 Ferrari 275 GTB/4-cam to Nicholas, but offered a condition in writing that transfer of title was contingent upon agreeing that he would drive only on Saturdays while sunny with the temperature ranging from 65-75°F, is limited to 100 miles per day, and cannot exceed 75 mph. Let us also assume that Nicholas agrees to this "contract." Once title of ownership is transferred to Nicholas, he becomes the owner, and Roger is no different than any other individual on the planet. By what right or authority does Roger, or anyone else, have to dictate to Nicholas how he uses his Ferrari, over which he has 100% ownership of title? The answer is exactly none. Certainly Roger would be well within his rights as an individual to recommend to Nicholas how he should use his newly acquired property and even document those recommendations on paper. He would likewise be well within his rights to require Nicholas to sign that document as a condition of transferring the title. What Roger does not have the right to do, however, is attempt to force Nicholas' compliance with those recommendations, even if outlined in the signed document. Any notion of contract is invalid on its face, since only the property owner has dominion over his property. Since Roger has no claim of title over the Ferrari any longer, he likewise has no claim over its use. Should Roger attempt to use coercion, his actions would violate Nicholas' natural rights and would therefore be criminal under natural law.

If Roger wishes to retain control over the Ferrari, he has two means by which he can accomplish this. The first was alluded to earlier by merely leasing his Ferrari to Nicholas. Since title of a lease is still fully retained by the property owner, any and all conditions he sets must be adhered to by Nicholas. The other means by which Roger could establish restrictions on use, albeit to a lesser degree, would be if he sold equity to Nicholas, making him a joint owner. This would invariably come with a contract stipulating not only the amount of equity to be sold, but also outlining the powers and abilities Nicholas would have as minority owner.

With this scenario highlighting the fallacy and invalidity of "contracts" that allow individuals to have governance over property of which they do not have ownership, it is easy to understand why deed restrictions do not have standing. To translate what was previously stated, the deed restrictions in and of themselves are not violations of the property owner's rights, but it is the attempt to coerce the property owner into compliance that are. An HOA may establish whatever guidelines they wish property owners to adhere, but they may not attempt to use any means of force in order to garner the property owner's compliance.

What makes a valid contract under the laws of nature is the mutual exchange of property. What gives a valid contract authority is the mutual and voluntary agreement to all of the terms therein. Every contract should have stipulations outlining terms should the contract be breached, what constitutes satisfaction of terms, whether or not a means of termination without breach exists, etc. While certainly some contracts will be far more complex than others in an anarcho-capitalist society, the idea that contracts would exist everywhere is not any different to their existence today. Just as major corporations enter into lengthy contracts with other companies, you enter into multiple contracts every single day. By stopping at a fast food restaurant for a meal, for example, your receipt is the contract transferring title of ownership of your currency for the meal. In this sense, the theory of anarcho-capitalism may be summed up in a single sentence: The purely voluntary exchange of private property.

Private property is a very real and concrete idea under the laws of nature. Without the existence of private property, it is impossible to accuse anyone of theft, extortion, trespassing, or even violence. Every individual has a property claim over their own lives, and if property does not exist, then neither does one's claim over their life. Property and the voluntary exchange thereof is what differentiates a slave from a free individual. A slave does not have the recognition of property, nor title over his own life. Slavery, therefore, violates the laws of nature, as does the Marxist mantra of the abolition of private property. To simply acknowledge the natural right to property, respect each other's rightful claim over their own, and ensure sole dominion over your own are the first steps to establishing a foundation for a society free of tyranny, and is thus free of a state.

Chapter 12

The Privatization of Money

"Run for your life from any man who tells you that money is evil. That sentence is the leper's bell of an approaching looter. So long as men live together on earth and need means to deal with one another – their only substitute, if they abandon money, is the muzzle of a gun."
– Ayn Rand, *Atlas Shrugged*

My previous chapter on the Federal Reserve System highlighted the fallacies of the current monopoly of currency by the state, while also highlighting the historic problems the early United States had with keeping the dollar stable. What I did not touch on is what exactly money is. Money is not what you have been conditioned to believe. The notes that bear the faces of Washington, Jefferson, Lincoln, Hamilton, Jackson, Grant, and Franklin are not money; they are currency. Currency and money do have a lot in common. They are both standardized mediums of exchange for goods and services, but there is one very important difference between the two; longevity of value.

To understand the difference, let us examine the supply and demand graph, with which anyone who has taken any basic economics course should be familiar. The x-axis shows the quantity of a product, and the y-axis shows its price. Two lines intersect in the graph: the supply line from bottom left to top right, and the demand line from top left to bottom right.

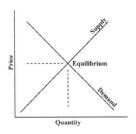

The point at which supply and demand meet is known as equilibrium (or competitive price). If supply were to increase while demand remains stagnant, then the price point must decrease to remain in equilibrium. The same would be true if the supply remains stagnant, but the demand were to decrease. This exact same economic law applies to currency and money as well. When the currency supply is arbitrarily increased, such as when the Treasury prints more notes, the value of the dollar decreases. Sure, it may still say $1 on the front and back, but that dollar buys less than it did before. While money is also subject to this, it stores its value far better than currency ever could. Effectively, there is an unlimited amount of currency since all it takes is running the printing press to make more of it, but since there is a finite amount of precious metals in the world, its value (in theory) only really fluctuates when new supplies are discovered or existing supplies are lost. We are getting ahead of ourselves though. We need to take a trip back to the first uses of money in order to understand how both money and currency came to exist.

In ancient times, bartering was the main means by which people exchanged goods, but the problem was determining whether the value of what was being offered was equal to the value you placed on what you were trying to sell. Are twenty ears of corn equal to five chickens? It really depends on a lot of factors, all of which can be completely independent of each other. These factors could be how badly you need chickens, how much value you put on chickens compared to corn, and the health and/or age of the chickens, etc. If you did not need chickens, then you have lost a sale simply because that was all he was able to offer for your corn. This is why money came into existence, but the question is why gold and silver became money.

John Locke essentially said that precious metals only have value because we have all arbitrarily agreed they do. In his words, "Gold, silver and diamonds, are things that fancy or agreement hath put the value on."[171] This is true to a large extent, but there is a reason that gold and silver are valuable beyond simply the fact that they are shiny metals. Precious metals have the perfect balance of three qualities that set them apart from other metals: scarcity, reactivity, and malleability.

---

171 Locke, John. (1689). *"Second Treatise of Government"*. Chapter V.

First and foremost, think back to the supply and demand chart and consider that gold is a scarce (rare) metal, but it is not the rarest of metals. That title belongs to rhodium, so why is rhodium not the standard? Anything that is too rare makes it useless as a medium of exchange. Rhodium's entire existence is estimated to be only three parts per billion (0.0000003%) in the entire universe. Sure, the universe is the largest place we know of, so such a tiny percentage should be taken with a grain of salt, right? Well, on the flip side, metals like aluminum and iron make up about 8.1% in the universe and 5% of the earth's crust.[172] If rhodium were to be money, very few would have it, and its value would be astronomical (it actually sits at around $8,300 per troy ounce). Aluminum, on the other hand, would be worthless due to its abundance. This is why gold was the global standard. It is rare enough to have value but not so scarce that only the most elite in the world can possess it. Even today, gold sits at around $1,900 per troy ounce, and fractional weights are sold all the way down to the gram (or about 0.03 troy ounces).

The second thing that makes metals like gold so valuable is how stable of an element it is. It resists wear, oxidation, corrosion, and deterioration in its natural state, which means that it withstands the test of time. The last thing anyone wants their money to do is disappear, so if nature takes it away, it does not do anyone much good. Forgetting scarcity for the moment, iron rusts, mercury melts at room temperature, copper tarnishes, and magnesium explodes when it touches water. Gold really is an amazing element purely from the standpoint of chemistry because it easily withstands most of what nature and even men can throw at it.

All of that aside, gold is also a metal that is quite malleable and easy to work with, which is essential in making it into coins. Blacksmiths have molded iron and alloys for centuries because getting it to a red-hot temperature to forge with is relatively easy. Even melting iron entirely for casting is not difficult as its melting point is 1,538°C. Gold is actually easier to cast into coins as its melting point comes in at nearly 500°C below that, at 1,068°C. Platinum, by comparison, has a melting point of 1,768°C, and tungsten's is 3,422°C. While we have no issues

---

172 Gillespie, Claire. (April 10, 2018). "What is the Rarest Metal?". *Sciencing*.

today making metals bend to our will due to technological advances, in 500 BCE, it was quite the different story. Gold was the perfect metal, with the perfect balance of scarcity, reactivity, and malleability to use as a medium of exchange. Silver shares a lot of these same qualities, which is why it usually accompanies gold in its regard as money. Platinum is a relatively recent discovery, as it was not really acknowledged by scientists until 1748.

Currency differs from money in the aspect that currency is merely a representation of money, not money itself. This is why early silver and gold certificates issued by the Treasury were redeemable for actual physical money. Currency was supposed to be a means of convenience and security for people engaging in trade, but has since become a means of economic destruction. Because money is finite, its value is held far more stable than that of currency. A currency's value cannot ever be stable, as its ability to be created out of nothing and counterfeited are the very thing that drives its instability. When the Fed prints more notes, the supply increases, thus diluting the dollar's buying power.

This answers the supply question as to how money and a currency's values are determined, but how does demand affect it and what exactly is buying power? After all, the demand for money or currency should be ever present, correct? The word "demand" correctly describes what happens in free market commerce but does not really describe what is actually happening as it relates to the dollar itself. The supply and demand graph should therefore be slightly altered:

If the supply line is the amount of currency in circulation, then the demand line is the people's confidence in that currency. The point at which these two lines intersect is the buying power of that currency. When people lack confidence in a nation's currency due to factors such as outside manipulation and control from the Federal Reserve, the demand to use that currency as a medium of exchange drops. This decreases the buying power of the currency, the same way a decrease in demand with a rising or stagnant supply would do in a free market. Since a money's supply cannot be arbitrarily created like a currency's supply can, this explains why money holds its value and currency does not.

Today, there is a new form of money that has taken the world by storm and caused a panic from the state: cryptocurrency (which by technicality should be called cryptomoney, but I digress). The invention of cryptocurrencies such as Bitcoin relinquished the state's firmly held monopoly on money, and despite their best efforts to push propaganda demonizing it, it became wildly popular. Despite its intangibility, cryptocurrency holds value the same way gold and silver specie do. There is a level of scarcity that cryptocurrency inventors have to create along with their privatized money supply in order for it to hold any value at all. The scarcity of any reputable cryptocurrency cannot be altered once it is set, though it can be "mined" into existence with high-powered computers solving incredibly complex math equations that grow exponentially more complex as each one is solved.

The creation of cryptocurrency reprivatized the control of money, which is where the power of money always should have been. The state's control over a money supply is the very reason problems with money exist. In ancient times, gold was accepted everywhere. Even if it was not paid in official specie minted by the state, trinkets and décor would be accepted if their weight in gold was enough to settle the debt. In an anarcho-capitalist society, private money would be the medium of exchange. Cryptocurrency has already established a means of security in the form of blockchain, which validates transactions and prevents the double-spending problem. This was developed entirely without involvement from the state. The only reason cryptocurrencies like Bitcoin are as volatile as they are in the market is because their prices are relative to the faith in the state's currency.

If state currencies were to be abolished entirely, cryptocurrencies and precious metals would become the standard mediums of exchange.

Private businesses would have the means of determining in which monies they wished to deal, and they would likely have a large selection from which their customers could choose. Currently, there are hundreds of cryptocurrencies available including Bitcoin, Ethereum, Zilliqa, and Chainlink. There are also a variety of private mints that mint coins from various precious metals, such as Sunshine Minting, Texas Precious Metals, Scottsdale Mint, and Golden State Mint. These are but a few examples but prove that the future of money in an anarcho-capitalist society would be secure. In today's society, it is essentially guaranteed that cryptocurrency would become the main medium of exchange due to its digital existence, which makes it the most convenient to use. While it may be daunting to think about hundreds of cryptocurrencies, the market would determine which ones succeed and which ones fail. The competition of the marketplace would ensure high amounts of security and even more innovation than is available even today.

Compared to the current state of currency (which is abysmal), market control in an anarcho-capitalist society would result in an incredibly stable state of money. The additional printing of currency to control the market would no longer exist as only the scarcity of cryptocurrency and precious metals would determine the valuation. There would be no need for a central bank, and the state would not exist to rob you of the value of your savings and income. Reminiscing about days of old where $5 would buy x or $10 would buy y would be over, as the dominant money as determined by the market would effectively make problems like devaluation and inflation a thing of the past. When one cryptocurrency begins to decline, another would take over as the dominant money. Fully privatizing money is how every individual can absolutely secure their financial futures for themselves. Liberty cannot exist without the full control of money residing in the hands of the individual who carries it.

Chapter 13

Justice Without Rulers

"Justice will not be served until those who are unaffected are as outraged as those who are." – Benjamin Franklin

J ustice has been a part of the American mantra since its inception, and when propaganda pushes the narrative that the state is necessary for the execution of justice, it implies that justice will not exist in a stateless society. Though it is widely believed that a state of anarchy equates to a state of chaos without rules, and while such a state *can* theoretically exist in anarchy, the word itself is defined incorrectly. The word *anarchy* is derived from the ancient Greek root arkhḗ (ἀρχή) meaning "leader" or "ruler." Adding the suffix -íā transforms arkhḗ into arkhíā (ἀρχίᾱ), which is the ancient Greek word for "government" or "state." This word evolved into the Greek word hierarkhía (ἱεραρχία), which is from where today's English word *hierarchy* comes. The Greek prefix a- or an- simply applies the negative. Therefore the true meaning of *anarchy* is "without rulers," ergo anarchy is the only means by which individualism is possible.

Throughout history, absolutists and monarchs of hierarchal states proved countless times to be antithetical to liberty and individualism. In modern history, republics and democracies have merely changed the structure of the hierarchy to give the illusion of liberty without actually changing the end result. This is why statists twisted the definition of anarchy from that of self-ownership and individualism to mean lawless chaos. The unfounded fears around a lack of security the state supposedly provides are what is necessary to keep the people in the bondage of slavery to the state. Nothing has truly changed from the monarchs of societies past to today's constitutional republics. We the people are nothing more than free-range peasants. The biggest selling point from the statist propaganda surrounding their necessity is that of justice. This has been so effective that many cannot comprehend any semblance of justice existing in a stateless society. It is incredibly possible, however.

What exactly is justice, though? Is justice punitive or rehabilitative? The simplest philosophical answer, as alluded to in chapter 7, is that justice is the means by which an individual who was victim to a criminal act is made whole again. The problem, however, is that no victim can ever truly be made whole again. Even a thief that steals $100 from someone cannot make his victim whole by returning the $100 back to him. The experience of being a victim in and of itself makes this an impossibility. It is even more apparent the more egregious the crime. A rape victim can never have the trauma they suffered undone, and a murder victim cannot have their life returned to them. True justice, therefore, does not exist as it is a manmade construct designed to be the means of protection for liberty. If a statist society cannot perfect man's own construct, how could a stateless society fare any better?

While justice in its true form does not exist, something reminiscent of justice does exist in an anarcho-capitalist society. First, we must establish as to what is the enforcement mechanism. Obviously, a stateless society of any kind will not have socialized law enforcement. As we have already established, the anarcho-capitalist society will have all property either privately owned or owned by nature. Also, as previously established, each property owner, particularly if they open their property for public use, would establish terms of use, which would define penalties for violating those terms. For example, let us pretend that Weiland Highway Company owns a 187-mile stretch of Interstate 10 in Texas stretching from Exit 556A on the east side of San Antonio to Exit 743A on the east side of Katy. Weiland Highway utilizes an RFID permit tag system for billing (similar to today's toll tags), posts speed limit signs designating a maximum speed of 85mph, and posts all of their policies and schedule of fees for violations on their public website (which must be agreed to for issuance of their permit tag). To enforce these policies, Weiland Highway contracts Smith Security Solutions to patrol that stretch of highway for trespassers without an RFID tag and to enforce their blood-alcohol limit policies. Weiland also contracts out Huntington Radars to establish speed enforcement cameras tied in with RFID tag readers for simple billing of fees.

While this seems simple enough for issues of speeding or even driving under the influence, how would this apply to the everyday individual merely seeking to stay protected? Rothbard suggested that one's homeowner's insurance company would likely create their own security subsidiary charged with protecting that which they insure, and that is certainly a brilliant idea. Even if State Farm did not create State Farm Security as a subsidiary, they would likely contract out another security company as part of their selling point. Like a good neighbor, State Farm is there with Delta Security's around-the-clock protection. In a more modern line of thought, security companies like ADT would likely be the ones to fill this need. It would even be possible for State Farm to partner with ADT to protect the property they are insuring. Regardless, the notion of a dispatcher answer the emergency line with "9-1-1, what is your credit card number?" is one that would *not* come to fruition.

These companies would have a fiduciary duty to their customers to not only do everything possible to recover any lost property, but also to protect the life of their client. Police today do not have such a duty, legal or otherwise. A municipal police officer in today's society does not have any motivation to ensure customer satisfaction. The best they can offer is filing a report that ultimately goes nowhere. In fact, only about 4.4% of all stolen household goods are recovered by law enforcement. Of all stolen properties in the U.S., vehicles are the most commonly recovered property at 56.1%, and miscellaneous property comes in 2nd at a recovery rate of just 12.9%.[173]

So, how would justice actually work in an anarcho-capitalist society? While there are countless ways, here is a basic anecdotal example. Let us establish a few things as fact for this scenario:

---

173 Recovery Rate of Stolen Property in the United States in 2019, by type (September 2020). Retrieved from https://www.statista.com/statistics/252444/recovery-rate-of-stolen-property-in-the-us-by-type/

- Bill did in fact murder Nancy.
- Nancy did nothing offensively aggressive to justify Bill's use of force against her.
- The evidence that is collected during the investigation can definitively prove Bill's guilt.
- Nancy is a client of Bulldog Security, and Bill is a client of Delta Security.

Whitney comes home after work to discover her roommate, Nancy, laying lifeless in a pool of her own blood. Panicking, she calls the emergency service line to Bulldog Security, her service provider. Bulldog investigators arrive, and follow all protocols for a proper investigation. They conclude that Nancy's ex-boyfriend, Bill Cunningham, who resides at 123 Spooner St., is their prime suspect and recommend an indictment against him. Bulldog prosecutors file for an indictment in Adler Jurisprudence Company (AJC) courts against Bill. AJC reviews the evidence and decides enough evidence is present to indict. They immediately mail Bill a Notice of Indictment, complete with the date and time for his arraignment in court. Where this differs from today is that no coercion is used in Bill's trial. Today, when charges are levied against an individual, they are immediately arrested and arraigned. This violates the individual's rights as they are coerced into compliance without voluntarily agreeing to it. In our scenario, Bill does not have to appear at his own trial. Should he fail to appear, then he cannot provide a defense for the adjudicators, who must therefore conclude he is guilty. Let us assume he contacts his service provider Delta Security to investigate, and Delta defense attorneys serve as his council during trial. The facts and evidence are argued, and the verdict comes down as guilty.

What happens next? Most people, including Rothbard, believe that once someone has been determined to have violated the rights of others, that they have forfeit their rights. I do not subscribe to this philosophy, as this makes natural rights no different than arbitrary privileges bestowed upon us by the state. Rights and liberty are perfect ideals, as they are inherent to us as human beings. Just as someone cannot give up their own genetics, it is impossible for one to surrender their rights.

This can be illustrated in binary where 1 equals one individual with their natural rights. Should 5 individuals exist with pure liberty as in an anarcho-capitalist society, the equation would be simply:

$$1 + 1 + 1 + 1 + 1$$

Should one individual commit an act that violates the liberty of another, the number can no longer be 1 and therefore must become 0. The caveat expressed at the end of liberty's definition in chapter 1, excepting acts that infringe on the rights of another, is not an arbitrary creation of my own design, and this can be proven with this same mathematical illustration. If one of the 5 individuals in this example murders another, the expression becomes:

$$1 + 1 + 1 + 1 + (1 - 1)$$

Which reduces down to:

$$1 + 1 + 1 + 1 + 0$$

The parenthetical expression exists to illustrate that the individual had liberty but then had it taken from him. First, notice that by this expression, you cannot tell which one of the other 4 actually committed the murder. This is because despite taking away the 5th individual's right to life, the aggressor does not have rightful claim of ownership to it. This is an impossibility, just as surrendering one's rights are. Several things are proven by this, though I will only stick to what is relevant here; first, because the negative exists in the expression, liberty's definition cannot include any act that infringes on the liberty of another, thus proving the aforementioned caveat. The second thing that is proven is that even though the guilty individual committed this act that violated the other person's liberty, his rights still exist, proving that one cannot surrender them. This binary equation ultimately illustrates the perfection of nature's liberty.

The question remains, though, as to how a guilty individual should be handled in an anarcho-capitalist society. Though it is not lost on me that implementing the pure philosophy of liberty will require a massive shift in cultural beliefs, no single aspect is more apparent than as it relates to the cultural views on criminal justice. Most small issues that would be tried in civil courts today could be handled without any real issue. Torts such as overdue highway tolls, or even whatever fines levied against an individual for drunk driving could be simply handled by asking their employer to garnish their wages, as an example. The solution to handling egregious criminal acts, however, will not be a popular one. Since the philosophy of natural rights requires the acknowledgment that rights cannot be usurped or surrendered, holding this principle consistently across all issues would seem on its face to mean that a serial killer would have nothing done to him, since he cannot be coerced into complying with anything with which he does not wish to comply. That is *technically* true; however, there is a valid means of "punishment" that would not directly violate such a criminal's rights.

One of the biggest cultural shifts that would have to be made in this area would be the media no longer making criminal proceedings public. This could not be coerced into compliance, but if adopted, would make this solution work. This solution would require the media to change its culture and not report the identity of any suspects for any criminal acts until *after* the trial concludes with a guilty verdict. Going back to Bill's murder of Nancy, once he is found guilty, the media reporting his picture, name, and even address would not be a violation of his rights, as this is all information that is easily accessible. The entire investigative reports could even be released. Exposing all of the details about what Bill did to Nancy would destroy his life. His employer would instantly terminate him. If he is renting his residence, his landlord could evict him, and he would likely have a target painted on his back from the public. Should Nancy's brother John decide to seek vengeance against Bill and murder him, this act of aggression certainly would violate Bill's rights, but there is a nice little byproduct created in this society.

John would likely get brought up on charges for homicide, and he might even show up to court to publicly proclaim his guilt, but the fallout could be very different for him. The public could view his actions as "justifiable" (or at least understandable) despite them clashing with the laws of nature. In effect, society would nullify his murder conviction, and his life would continue on as normal. Would this be unfair to Bill's family? Absolutely, but equality is not a natural right.

Many might attempt to label this as a form of vigilante justice, but I absolutely reject such a label. It is the capitalist society that would derive the solution to establish a system of justice, and should it establish this very system, it would not be the system that was responsible for the assault on Bill's rights. John acted alone, and there is no guarantee that he would have acted at all. Nothing compelled him to do so. Moreover, there is also no guarantee that society would nullify John's actions as was done in our previous scenario. They may choose to societally and culturally destroy him as they did Bill before his murder. One thing that may not be a guarantee, but is incredibly likely, is that scenarios such as the one outlined above would make infringing on other people's rights a highly undesirable act to commit. Cases of homicide, rape, and assault would likely become incredibly rare, even more than they are today.

Another major benefit to the full privatization of the justice system would be the on the issue of police brutality. Because "cops" in an anarcho-capitalist society would only be able to serve in an investigative capacity or respond to an active threat on private property, their station would be equal to that of everyone else. Any notion or semblance of qualified immunity or powers superior to that of the private individual would not exist. Should a security agent act in a criminal manner under the laws of nature, he would be held to exactly the same standards as everyone else. He would not have the authority to act in a manner that is justifiable for him but criminal to someone else.

Privatizing the entire justice system would make it streamlined and more efficient, as competition and market needs would supply a demand, ultimately resulting in an all-around better world. The idea that anarchy would be chaotic would prove to be false. Take a step back and ask yourself why you do not commit crimes (as defined by the laws of nature). Is it because the state tells you not to? It is probably more likely that you would not engage in those acts even if we lived in a state of anarchy. Ask that same question of your friends, family, and neighbors. Chances are, the overwhelming majority of people you know (if not all of them) would answer the latter. Moreover, more people would take personal responsibility for their own security and arm themselves. This would further reduce violations of natural law to a near-negligible amount. The truth of an anarcho-capitalist society is that it would not be a swill of vigilante justice and nonstop violence. It would likely be the state of peace that every statist strives to achieve through coercion and a monopoly on violence. This is not to say such a society would be utopian but rather is a realistic solution to dealing with whatever criminal element that would be present in any society while preserving everyone's natural rights. After all, justice cannot exist in a state of tyranny.

Chapter 14

Protecting Nature's Treasures

"Look deep into nature, and then you will understand everything better."
– Albert Einstein

There is a stigma surrounding capitalism that is the result of collectivist propaganda. The image of the billionaire scoffing at the peasants as he dumps toxic waste into a clean river while simultaneously taking joy in watching them starve to death is one many, particularly of the leftist ideology, conjure when they think of the capitalist. This is the way Marx painted them (calling them bourgeoisie), and this image is what many on the socialist spectrum believe to be true. Fortunately, this image is the very opposite of what any good capitalist, or even the most greedy and self-important capitalist, would want.

There are many who will focus more on environmental concerns of unregulated (true) capitalism than the idea of peasants starving in the streets as a result of capitalist greed. In reality, this is far more of a rational concern that the statist would have when compared to the latter, but it is still not one that needs a coercive force to achieve. Regardless of where one stands on the issues of climate change, it cannot be argued that the original environmental harms caused by industry were done so as a result of malicious intent. At its worst, these original harms were committed far more out of ignorance than out of malice.

Many might believe the notion that an anarcho-capitalist society would revert to businesses dumping toxic sludge into rivers and streams; however, this idea is devoid of an understanding of profit motive. Much like the example used regarding discrimination in Part I, the market and natural law would have control over environmental protections. Since all land would either be privately owned or belong to nature, environmental harms would have a direct impact on surrounding property owners, thereby violating the laws of nature. Let us assume for the moment that Martin Chemical owns and operates a chemical plant on a 1200-acre plot of land. Should their production produce toxic vapors, for example, their employees would likely expose their unsafe work practices publicly, thereby applying pressure on any contractual partners with Martin Chemical, and thus placing their future in severe jeopardy. If employees also quit en masse, their operations would be forced to cease, putting the company in a state of certain failure.

What if, however, instead of making their employees sick from toxic fumes, they were ordered to bury toxic byproducts that were benign to humans, but toxic to the ground once buried? This answer depends on one very important factor: whether or not the environmental damage extend beyond the boundaries of their property line. If it does, then surrounding property owners would have a legitimate claim of aggression against Martin Chemical. Bear in mind that in an anarcho-capitalist society, the court system would be entirely privately owned and operated, thereby leveling the playing field between Martin Chemical's 5.2 million Ethereum (or $10 billion) company and Bill Cunningham's 130 Ethereum ($250,000) estate. Martin Chemical attorneys would not have convoluted laws and the ability to financially drain Bill's wealth by dragging out proceedings. Moreover, Bill's property insurance company would likely spearhead his claim, as they have a financial motivation to do so. Should the court find Martin Chemical guilty of destroying part of Bill's property, they could voluntarily negotiate punitive damages or go public with the details of the case.

On the other hand, if all of the toxic waste that Martin Chemical buried on their property had no effect on surrounding properties, then this is entirely their right to do. No one would argue that the felling of trees, the leveling of the land, and the building of a structure on virgin land is not destructive to that environment. It absolutely is destructive in its very essence, yet this is how all of society has been created, and is how title of property ownership gets transferred from nature's ownership to the new owner. If Martin Chemical rightfully owned the property under which they buried the toxic waste, they are doing no more environmental damage than had been done when constructing their chemical plant or when John Cunningham built his home next door. It may be upsetting to some outsiders, but taking issue with how one utilizes their own property is not grounds for encroaching on their rights.

This brings us to the question of nature's most beautiful places, what we call national and state parks. These areas of minimally tarnished land are truly gorgeous specimens to behold. The state preserves these specimens as a means of protecting them from man's development, and thus many believe that an anarcho-capitalist society would see the areas of the Grand Canyon, the Rocky Mountains, Yosemite, and other federally protected lands comprising about 28% of the United States' 2.27 billion acres be industrialized or developed.[174] While this could theoretically happen, there is an exponentially greater chance that these parks would become privately owned and operated. There is a huge financial incentive for private companies to preserve areas of nature for the purposes of retaining their natural beauty, and even for camping, fishing, and hunting.

There is one aspect that seems to be lost in the debate of what would happen to national parks should the state be abolished: population density. If the entire global population were gathered in a single area and concentrated at the same density as San Francisco, the area would only be about the size of Texas, Oklahoma, Arkansas, and Louisiana combined, or 398,000 square miles.[175] While this of course excludes any and all agricultural requirements to sustain the population, it is indicative of just how much living space there is on the planet for all of us, even with our record population. Most of the land area comprising the national parks are not ideal areas for farming, as they are either in the mountains or in the desert. The other lands that could have potential farm use would likely not be utilized that way simply because these areas have become sacred in the eyes of the people. If the state were entirely abolished across the United States of America, current parks like Yosemite and Redwood National Park would be almost instantly brought under the management and ownership of private companies. The best part for nature lovers is

174 Federal Land Ownership: Overview and Data. (February 21, 2020). *Congressional Research Service.* Retrieved from https://fas.org/sgp/crs/misc/R42346.pdf
175 De Chant, Tim (January 18, 2011). "If the World's Population Lived in One City". *Per Square Mile.* Retrieved from https://persquaremile.com/2011/01/18/if-the-worlds-population-lived-in-one-city/

that the profit motive behind the preservation of these parks would yield a far better experience and means of protection than the state ever could dream of producing.

How does this fall in line with the laws of nature, though? After all, unless labor is mixed with a piece of property, it rightfully belongs to nature, and the entire purpose of these types of parks is to preserve the way nature has given it to us. By technicality under the laws of nature, the entirety of the park would *not* be owned by whichever company claims ownership of it. There would no doubt be areas that either cannot be made into trails for hikers to follow, or will not allow for any markers whatsoever to be laid. No fencing would be put up around the entirety of the land, and any wanderer might believe himself to be on natural land and inadvertently be trespassing. This should be of no concern, as it is not an issue even today. A significant part of the American culture has a major appreciation for the national parks. Data from 2019 shows that all national parks have over 327 million visitations and nearly 14 million overnight stays annually.[176] Because of this cultural appreciation of nature, even though a private company's ownership of the entirety of a national park would not technically be recognized by the laws of nature, their claim of ownership would be recognized by the various societies surrounding those parks. In the event of a dispute involving private courts, the cultural (market) pressures surrounding the preservation of these areas would lead the courts to recognize their claims as well. If the claim of ownership did need to be argued on the grounds of natural law, the argument could be levied that because the enjoyment of all of the property to the most virgin land is the epitome of the property owner's business venture, even simply due to spectators coming to view it, that satisfies the requirement of mixing one's labor with the land. This, however, would be a bit of a stretch, but the argument could be made if needed.

Another major cultural appreciation is that of hunting and fishing, which also coincides with conservation efforts. The overwhelming majority of hunters and fishermen have a profound understanding of the needs of conservation, and many use their passion for wildlife conser-

---

176 "National Park Visitations Tops 327 Million in 2019". (February 27, 2020). Retrieved from https://www.nps.gov/orgs/1207/2019-visitation-numbers.htm

vation as their motivations for engaging in such activities. While many use the eradication of the buffalo as the rationale behind state-issued hunting and fishing licenses (and this was certainly a lesson learned), the necessity behind these licenses is for naught. Since all property would be privately owned or belong to nature, "unregulated" hunting would not result in a repeat of the buffalo eradication.

The term *unregulated* was put in quotes because though the state would not exist in an anarcho-capitalist society, and therefore the non-existent state could not regulate hunting and fishing, the owners of each and every lease could not only regulate hunting on their property, but their profit motive and fiduciary duty to the market would insist that they do. Should a property owner not care about wildlife conservation in any way yet still enter into the business of hunting leases, it would still behoove him to establish bag limits, as well as criteria on which wildlife may be hunted and when. This is simply due to the fact that whatever game he offers becomes his product. No matter what business one runs, ensuring a supply to meet the demand is essential, and hunting or fishing leases are not exempt from this criterion.

This raises the question as to animal rights. Many libertarian philosophers, including Rothbard and Walter Block, denounce the notion of animals having rights, but that is a position with which I disagree. In nature, many animal species have shown to exercise the exact same natural rights as we have as human beings. The right to life goes without saying, as animals will do anything within their power to preserve their own lives and even defend the lives of their young. No one could argue against a wild animal's right to liberty, as they do invoke sole dominion over their lives. Even the right to property is displayed by many of the more intelligent wild species.

As a stunning example of this, a study was conducted by the Voyageurs Wolf Project in 2015 where the team tagged seven alpha male wolves in northern Minnesota with GPS trackers. These trackers recorded their positions every 20 minutes for about 7 weeks, resulting in approximately 68,000 GPS data points for each wolf. When their positions were plotted on a map, seven clearly defined territories were revealed, all of which were adjacent to one another. With the exception of some very slight overlap, these wolves never entered into another wolf's domain.[177] This is clearly indicative of these wolves establishing title of ownership over that territory. It also absolutely fits the requirement under the laws of nature to claim such title of ownership. While these wolves may not be tilling fields, sowing seeds, or raising structures for shelter on their lands, the fact that they are patrolling their territory hunting game for sustenance is unquestionably the act of mixing their labor with the land.

Photo credit: Voyageurs Wolf Project.
Edited to highlight boundaries in grayscale

What of the other animals in that territory? Do they have the claim of ownership over that property as well? It entirely depends upon their nature. If they are territorial by nature, absolutely. If are a nomadic species, then any individual would undoubtedly have the right to claim ownership over property should it choose to defy its nature and become territorial. Nomadic species should not be thought of as being without the right to property but merely a species whose nature chooses to not lay claim to property, the same way an individual man chooses to live a nomadic lifestyle traveling the wilderness. He has no territorial property,

---

177 Johnson, Stephen. (April 16, 2019). "GPS Data Shows How Wolf Packs Carve out Territory". *Big Think*. Retrieved from https://bigthink.com/surprising-science/wolf-gps

just as the nomadic animal species does not, because he chose not to claim any. The same logic holds true for migratory species that establish temporary properties, such as for nesting young, and then subsequently abandon their nests.

The former point, of course, might seem confusing if two species both claim ownership over the same piece of territory. After all, if the property is owned by one, no other may lay claim of ownership, correct? The solution to this is a philosophical theory which I call the interspecies property ownership theory. Put simply, this theory essentially establishes that any territorial property may be owned under the laws of nature by multiple species. As an example, if a female cardinal builds a nest in a tree in your back yard, the interspecies property ownership theory concludes that this nest is the property of the cardinal despite being in a tree that is your property. You will likely pay it no mind and might even put out a bird bath and feeder to subsidize the new cardinal family until they migrate away.

Does this mean that you as the owner of the tree cannot cut it down or even simply destroy the nest, so long as the cardinal occupies it? Not at all. The interspecies property ownership theory still recognizes the predator/prey relationship established by nature. This relationship allows for the unprovoked killing of animals for the purposes of sustenance. This is what justifies humans hunting of game or fishing and even justifies the raising of cattle for slaughter. While sport killing, or killing for fun, has been observed in more than a few species of animals (particularly among felines, including your pet cat), these killings violate the deceased animal's rights; however, since every non-human species lacks the intellectual capacity to understand concepts such as natural law and natural rights, they have no means by which to offer recourse to any victim (hence why justice is a manmade construct). What does all of this mean for the cardinal whose nest you destroyed? If you destroyed it because you enjoy eating cardinal eggs or killed the cardinal because you wanted to utilize its feathers in decorating a hat, you would be justified under nature's predator/prey relationship. Should you kill the cardinal for sport or simply cut down the tree ignorant of her nest's existence, you would have violated the rights of the cardinal; however, many will likely conclude that this means you would be a criminal in an anarcho-capitalist society, but they should not.

Recall from the previous chapter the foundational example I provided for the privatized justice system for a moment. When Whitney discovered the lifeless body of her roommate, Nancy, she had called her security company to launch the investigation, which subsequently led to charges being levied against her ex-boyfriend, Bill. In our current scenario, who is going to be the one to file charges against you for killing the cardinal? Certainly the cardinal's mate or young could not, as they lack the intellectual capacity to do so. What if your neighbor witnessed you murder the cardinal from his own property though? Calling his security company or even yours (assuming it is a different company, and he is knowledgeable of this fact) would prove to be useless, as they would have no authority in such matters. If he went straight to the court to petition them for charges, chances are his petition would be viewed as a waste of their resources. Should they actually indict you and find you guilty, or should your neighbor simply post a video of you killing the cardinal on social media, the kickback would likely be minimal. Had it been a wasp nest or ant bed that you destroyed, you would be hard pressed to find anyone who held anything remotely resembling contempt for your actions. On the other hand, should your neighbor witness you needlessly killing a stray dog, the outcome would likely be very different due to our cultural love for them.

The rationale behind expounding on (or even acknowledging) the rights of animals despite the near-zero likelihood of measurable consequences for abusing most species in an anarcho-capitalist society is not done out of altruism. It is necessary for two reasons. The first is to remain intellectually consistent. If my chastising of the state for placing themselves in a superior station to us and refusing to acknowledge our natural rights is followed by a belief that animals do not have rights because their species are factually subservient to human beings, then I view that as holding two inconsistent positions. While I personally find it immoral to harm a dog that is not aggressing against you and simultaneously see no moral issue whatsoever with murdering an entire ant bed in my front yard, they are both the same from a philosophical standpoint. My moral compass is independent from my philosophical beliefs, as all of ours should be. The second reason, and more important one, is to reinforce the philosophy behind our natural rights. Highlighting examples of property ownership in the animal kingdom, as with the wolves in Minnesota, is a fantastic way to help reinforce property ownership as a natural right to anyone who might take issue with nature as its arbiter. While not all animal species are territorial by nature, all territorial species lay claim to property, to include human beings.

Despite the negative light in which socialists paint capitalists, the fact remains that capitalism is driven by a combination of both profit and passion. For the entrepreneur, there is a huge profit to be made in the preservation of natural treasures, like Yosemite, as well as the preservation and control of hunting. For those that have passion alongside profit propelling their motivations, they stand a greater likelihood of success than one with profit as their sole motivator. Many people within the United States would happily take on the venture of preserving our national parks and wildlife due to their love for both. While investors who finance these ventures might be solely profit driven, with the passionate conservationist at the helm, and the investor navigating, it is that love that will help raise the standards in conservation efforts across the globe. This is only possible in an anarcho-capitalist society, as the state has no true motivations for either. It was the late Steve Irwin's passion, and that of his wife and children, that helped turn Australia Zoo into the icon of wildlife conservation that it is today. Imagine how amazing Australia Zoo would be if the state's restrictions did not prevent them from operating the ways they know are best. Now imagine that same thing applied to the beautiful national parks and game management. The only way to ensure the protection of nature's treasures is done as effectively and as efficiently as possible is with the elimination of the hindrance that is state. For those truly passionate about nature, the only solution is anarcho-capitalism.

Chapter 15

Liberty: The Good, the Bad, and the Ugly

"A man's natural rights are his own, against the whole world; and any
infringement of them is equally a crime... whether committed by one man,
calling himself a robber, or by millions calling themselves a government."
– Lysander Spooner

I n the opening chapter of this treatise, I stated that liberty in her true
form insinuated "that others will act in a manner with which you
will personally disagree; sometimes, even to a deplorable, and morally abhorrent level." It is now time to come full circle and show what
liberty looks like in all of her colors. An anarcho-capitalist society is in no
way utopian. There are no guarantees for success despite one's hard work,
passion, motivations, or good deeds. Likewise, there are no guarantees for
truly repugnant individuals to fail and get what society believes they deserve. Anarcho-capitalism offers only one thing: a level playing field for all.
This, however, does not guarantee fairness from things beyond our control.

Imagine for the moment that you live in an anarcho-capitalist
society. In this place, the individual is sovereign over himself. No other
individual, or group of individuals, has even the perceived authority of
having more of a say over your life, your body, your property, and the
fruits of your labor than you as the individual do. You have sole dominion
over that which you own, and no entity exists with a monopolistic threat
of violence should you not comply with whatever arbitrary edict or fee
they levy against you. You outright own your home, keep 100% of your
wages, and the price of goods and services are not artificially inflated at
the point of sale, or by other arbitrary, nonessential costs rolled into the
price by the supplier. Private property is king, whether that be the modest

home someone worked hard to obtain, or a corporate empire created by a visionary in his garage decades earlier. You have total control over your money, real money. Your monetary choices are virtually endless, and you always have the option of dealing in physical precious metals should you so choose. There is no expectation of your savings devaluing every single year, and there is no centralized entity pulling the strings on some paper currency not worth the cotton on which it is printed. The roads are always in near-perfect condition, since failure to perform routine maintenance and repairs would cause the free market to react negatively and reduce profits for the owner. Your children's school is affordable due to competition, focuses on the curricula you find to be best for your children, and the quality of their education is exceptional.

While all of this is certainly positive, I do not paint this picture to suggest this is the life everyone will experience (though I do believe this will be far more common than not). There are certainly going to be those in society succumbing to dire circumstances due to sloth, poor decisions, and even simple bad luck. Some will be deserving of the destitute state in which they find themselves, while others will not. Fortunately, despite what socialists wish to believe, capitalism is the reason the world's most effective charities exist, even in today's society. In an anarcho-capitalist society, though, the effectiveness of charities will climb exponentially. Here is something to consider: compiling data from Giving USA, USGovernmentRevenue.com, The Tax Foundation, the IRS, and the Consumer Price Index Inflation Calculator, despite the number of taxpayers increasing by 150% between 1954 and 2016 and total government revenue (federal, state, and local) increasing by a massive 559% (after adjusting for devaluation, and totaling nearly 60% of the total adjusted gross income), charitable donations still increased by 622%![178, 179, 180, 181, 182]

178 Statistics on U.S. Generosity. (2019). *Philanthropy Roundtable*. Retrieved from https://www.philanthropyroundtable.org/almanac/statistics/u.s.-generosity
179 Individual Income Tax Returns for 1954. (1957). *Government Printing Office*. Retrieved from https://www.irs.gov/pub/irs-soi/54inar.pdf
180 Total Government Revenue in the United States Fiscal Year 1954. Retrieved from https://www.usgovernmentrevenue.com/total_1954USbt_22bs1n
181 Total Government Revenue in the United States Fiscal Year 2016. Retrieved from https://www.usgovernmentrevenue.com/total_2016USrt_22rs1n
182 Robert Bellafiore. (November 13, 2018). "Summary of the Latest Federal Income

	1954 (Adjusted)	2016	Increase
Adjusted Gross Income (AGI)	$ 2,053,888,899,628.25	$10,200,000,000,000.00	397%
Number of Taxpayers	56,300,000	140,900,000	150%
Average AGI/Taxpayer	$ 36,481.15	$ 72,391.77	98%
Total Tax Revenue	$ 910,063,717,472.12	$ 6,000,000,000,000.00	559%
Percentage of AGI	44.31%	58.82%	33%
Total Net Incomes (AGI-Revenue)	$ 1,143,825,182,156.13	$ 4,200,000,000,000.00	267%
Average Net Income/ Taxpayer	$ 20,316.61	$ 29,808.37	47%
Charitable Giving	$ 54,000,000,000.00	$ 390,000,000,000.00	622%
Charitable Giving/ Taxpayer	$ 959.15	$ 2,767.92	189%
Percentage of Avg Net Income	4.7%	9.3%	97%

An obvious correlation that can be easily drawn is due to the increase in average income. Average Adjusted Gross Income (AGI) per taxpayer increased by 98% from 1954 to 2016, and likewise, charitable giving as a percentage of each taxpayer's average net income increased by 97%. This is a definitive sign that the American culture is charitable by nature, especially when accounting for the fact that the average net income by taxpayer only increased by 47%. It is quite curious as to what speculative conclusions could be drawn by reimagining 2016's charitable America as an anarcho-capitalist society.

Analyzing the total government spending for that year at the federal, state, and local levels, an approximate total of $1.85 trillion was spent on the following necessities:

- Education
- Roads, Airports, and Rail
- Police and Fire Services

Tax Data, 2018 Update". Retrieved from https://taxfoundation.org/summary-latest-federal-income-tax-data-2018-update/

- Agriculture, Forestry, Land Conservation, Fish, and Game
- Waste Management
- Water, Electricity, and Gas Supply

For our speculative purposes, we will assume that the costs per taxpayer in 2016 is exactly the same as the costs of these services in our reimagined anarcho-capitalist society (despite the likelihood that these costs would be substantially lower due to competition). We will also assume the same "gross" income, and the same number of "taxpayers" (bear in mind that in our reimagined anarcho-capitalist society, all of the "tax revenue" is the result of voluntary exchange). Finally, we will adjust the total amount of charitable giving to match the same 9.3% of net income as was the case in 2016. Here is our reimagined 2016 summary:

	2016	2016 Reimagined
Adjusted Gross Income (AGI)	$ 10,200,000,000,000.00	$ 10,200,000,000,000.00
Number of Taxpayers	140,900,000	140,900,000
Average AGI/Taxpayer	$ 72,391.77	$ 72,391.77
Total Tax Revenue	$ 6,000,000,000,000.00	$ 1,850,000,000,000.00
Percentage of AGI	58.82%	18.14%
Total Net Incomes (AGI-Revenue)	$ 4,200,000,000,000.00	$ 8,350,000,000,000.00
Average Net Income/Taxpayer	$ 29,808.37	$ 59,261.89
Charitable Giving	$ 390,000,000,000.00	$ 780,000,000,000.00
Charitable Giving/Taxpayer	$ 2,767.92	$ 5,535.84
Percentage of Avg Net Income	9.3%	9.3%
Net Less Charity	$ 27,040.45	$ 53,726.05

In our reimagined anarcho-capitalist 2016, the amount of charitable donations doubled compared to its real world counterpart from $390 billion to $780 billion, as did our "net" income. Police, fire, parks, wildlife conservation, education, waste management, utilities, roads, bridges, and airports are still 100% funded based off of 2016 federal, state, and local spending (and are likely in far better condition than the real world). In spite of all of this, you are voluntarily utilizing these services without having your property extorted from you and your "net" income has doubled (a minor part of which comes from the abolition of sales taxes, import tariffs, and all other taxes that artificially increase the price of goods). This is a huge blessing not only for you, but for those that find themselves in a state of destitution. Charities would be far more effective than any state welfare program, as they would easily have double the resources to help people to get off the streets and back on their feet.

There are some major downsides, however. As I stated earlier, this is not a utopian idea. People *will* act in manners which many may find immoral. For example, there will be no controls over substances like methamphetamine, heroin, or cocaine. Without a doubt, some people will abuse these drugs as they have done both now with the war on drugs in full force, as well as before the state ever began to control them. Some people will also engage in acts that people who are religiously devout might have a problem with, such as prostitution, polyamory, or allowing their 8 year old to transition, and some property owners may discriminate against you on the basis of your individual qualities over which you may or may not have control. All of these things, both good and bad, are enshrined in our natural right to liberty, and they belong to each and every one of us regardless of our race, sex, religion, creed, sexual orientation, gender identity, and yes, even our age.

This brings me to a very difficult topic to discuss: children. I must preface this by stating affirmatively that I absolutely believe that human life begins at conception, and that parents are morally obligated to care for their children. Everything I am about to discuss, I find to be morally repugnant, and in some issues, I would label them as outright evil. Despite this affirmation, in order to remain intellectually consistent, I must also concede that abortion is absolutely a natural right. This, at first, seems to be absolutely antithetical positions one can hold. If life is a natural life, and human life begins at conception, how, under any form of sound logic, can the decision to abort a pregnancy, and thereby terminate a human life, be in and of itself a natural right?

To answer this, we must take a step back to ensure the context is properly established. Let us assume that your brother Brad is severely ill. Let us also establish it as matter of fact that you are literally the only person on earth who can properly care for him. Should anyone else attempt to, despite their best efforts, Brad will die. Brad being your brother, you voluntarily welcome him into your home to give him the vital treatment that he needs. For whatever reason, you decide at a later time to change your mind. The question is now raised as to whether you have the natural right to remove him from your property or simply cease providing him care, despite the fact that doing so will result in his death. Certainly doing so would be considered immoral by most people, but does it violate natural law? The answer is no. As an individual with sole dominion over your life and property, you are the ultimate authority as to who is welcome, and who is not. As owner of your body and labor, you likewise have the ultimate authority over which labor you perform and which labor you do not. You also retain the right to change your mind at any point and as many times as are possible.

If pro-lifers applied their position to this scenario, because you voluntarily agreed to take Brad in and care for him, you should now be forced under threat of violence to continue to provide for him both your property and your labor until they are either no longer required for his survival, or another becomes both capable and willing to take over your mandated duties. What has happened in this situation is that another individual has placed themselves in a superior station to you, and insisted that they have more of a say over your life, your property, and the fruits of your labor than you do. This transforms your relationship from voluntary caregiver to that of a slave (credit to Murray Rothbard for creating the foundation for this analogy). [183]

The same logic holds true for a woman who becomes pregnant. Every single individual has a property right over their own bodies, meaning just as they have the ultimate authority over everything within the boundaries of their territorial property, the same applies to everything happening within their bodies. Yes, a fertilized ova is a human life, and

183 Rothbard. (1982).

while that individual *does* have the natural right to live, he *does not* have the right to enslave anyone else, even if his life depends on it. I find it absolutely disheartening that no means of removing a nonviable child from his mother's womb without killing him exists, but nature does not amend the rights it bestows upon us based upon the current abilities of technology.

There is a popular creed among libertarians that they use as the litmus test for determining what an individual has the right to do, to which has been alluded throughout this treatise, called the nonaggression principle (NAP). In essence, the NAP is the belief that no one has the right to initiate an act of aggression against another. The issue of abortion has pro-life and pro-choice libertarians split on if the NAP applies to terminating a woman's pregnancy. Pro-life libertarians argue that since the unborn baby is not committing an act of aggression, and the act of terminating the pregnancy is an act of aggression, abortion therefore violates the NAP; ergo a woman does not have the right to an abortion.

This is a misapplication of the NAP however. While it is true that the unborn child is not guilty of any act of aggression against the mother as he did not choose to be in utero, the act of performing the abortion, though grotesque and aggressive by its nature, ultimately does not apply to the NAP. This is strictly due to the fact that no method exists for removing the unborn child from his mother's womb and allowing him to continue development. Should such a technique be developed, then any antiquated techniques resulting in the child's death *could* be in violation of the NAP, though this depends on other factors, such as the mother's financial ability to utilize this technology. Another exception to this would be if the modern technique which sustains the unborn child's life outside his mother's womb could only be performed past a certain gestational age, and the mother wished to abort her pregnancy before that threshold was reached.

There is another aspect to this that needs to be discussed, for which again I credit Murray Rothbard's analogy. The scenario involving your brother Brad seems to insinuate that there is no threshold by which natural law establishes a prohibition on abortion. This is true, and it also applies to children who are both in their third trimester, as well as children who have been born. Notice in the Brad scenario, no actual act of aggression was committed against him. It was your decision to merely stop providing him care that led to his demise that was deemed acceptable under natural law, and this is exactly what is meant by my previous statement of application to post-born children.

A child, from the moment he is conceived in the womb, is a unique individual and sole owner of himself. A child's parents do not own him, as he is not their property. Conceding that he is their property would make the child a slave to the parents. Conversely, as the parents are not the owner of their child, the parents bear no actual responsibility for their children under natural law, as conceding that they did would be to make the parents a slave to the child. Across the overwhelming majority of cultures globally, if not all, there is a de facto hierarchy established between parent and child, and I am in no way suggesting that we should change that nearly-global belief. I am, however, acknowledging that under natural law, this cultural belief has no real authority. Without a doubt, everyone (myself included) would find the act of a parent starving their newborn child to death to be labeled nothing short of pure evil; however, no individual is entitled to the labor or property of another, even if they are physically and mentally incapable of obtaining the basic necessity of water on their own. Ironically, despite the fact that a parent neglecting his child to death is a natural right (which could take a week or more of agony), should that same parent commit an aggressive act that kills his child instantly, he would be guilty of murder under natural law.

Thankfully, due to the cultural view of the relationship of parent and child globally, the odds of this act of pure, unadulterated evil ever tragically coming to pass in an anarcho-capitalist society would be just shy of zero. Should it happen, despite it not violating any natural law, it would be all but guaranteed that the parent or parents who neglected their child in such a way and allowed him to suffer an ungodly amount of pain and torture that he in no way was even able to attempt to comprehend would likely be publicly assassinated while society revered their executioner as a hero. In regards to abortion, society would culturally establish acceptable limits in which they would shame a woman for aborting her pregnancy beyond a certain gestational age.

There is one other issue surrounding children that we must examine, but again, I will reiterate my affirmative view that despite the content which this section contains, I am in no way desirous of changing our current cultural belief surrounding this topic; this is the issue of adulthood. Like the parent who starves their child to death, there is a special place in Hell for anyone who believes it is morally acceptable to engage in sex with individuals we culturally believe to be children. Again, citing the fact that every individual, regardless of their age, is the sole owner of themselves and responsible for any decisions they make, should an adolescent woman consent to sex with a middle aged man, this does not violate natural law. The argument from the standpoint of protecting the young woman with statist laws is that her naïveté resulting from her limited life experience means that she cannot properly give consent to the man, thereby concluding the man raped her. Fortunately, the spirit of these statist laws coincide with the cultural beliefs that would still exist in an anarcho-capitalist society surrounding this sort of relationship and would likely result in the male being publicly humiliated, if not fed into a wood chipper feet first by heavily armed individuals in Hawaiian shirts, depending on various factors.

Finally, we arrive at the outright ugly part of liberty. While this is far less philosophical, and far more speculative, it must be addressed. I unequivocally believe that an anarcho-capitalist society can function on a large scale in a desirable state of peace, and I do not believe that the establishment of the first anarcho-capitalist society would be born out of revolution. If another revolution take place in the United States, should the revolutionaries achieve victory, they would institute another statist society under the guise of preserving liberty. Their intentions would be pure, but their creation of a new state would instantly usurp every individual's natural rights the second it is conceived.

Revolutions are driven by a common, or similar enough ideology, and unfortunately for those of us currently of the anarcho-capitalist philosophy, our beliefs fit neither criteria when compared to the substantial majority of those who would be willing to overthrow the tyrannical state. This is overwhelmingly dominated by statist conservatives who view the state as an evil necessary for the preservation of liberty. They revere America's Founding Fathers as gods among men, and to their credit, they did pen the most amazing founding document of any nation that history had ever seen. While the modern conservative is substantially more statist than the Founding Fathers, should they overthrow the state and start again from scratch, the statist society which they create would be exponentially better than the current state of things. Unfortunately, this significantly smaller, yet still-big government nation would only grow more powerful every single day of its existence and would eventually become reminiscent of the very thing they fought to overthrow.

I fear that what would be required to institute the first truly anarcho-capitalist society would be far worse than the onset of war. I believe it would require a catastrophic event, such as a global economic collapse or a nuclear war. Hundreds of millions of people, if not north of one billion people, would die as a result of such an event due to most people's lack of preparedness and dependence upon existing supply chains for sustenance paired with widespread panic-induced violence. It would have to be out of this decimation that a society truly valuing real liberty, that is the anarcho-capitalist society, would be created, and that would only be so conceived due to anarcho-capitalist philosophers of the past.

It would start as a relatively small group of individuals, most of whom if not all, would have labeled themselves as anarcho-capitalists since before the onset of the catastrophe. They would unite as individuals striving for achieving a common goal, but be motivated by what they believe to be best for them individually instead of what is best for the collective. They would find a decimated city or town in which to establish their new society, and welcome others who wish to join. The anarcho-capitalist founders would spread their philosophies to the newcomers, and despite their uncertainty regarding it, they would do their best to voluntarily adapt to their culture.

As months turn into years, the once small settlement of only a few anarcho-capitalists would have grown, as those that came later would eventually grasp a full understanding of anarcho-capitalism in practice and experience its benefits and blessings for themselves. Word would travel about this settlement, and those who had once been unsure of the culture would be spreading the seeds of liberty to other newcomers. While some individuals would choose to violate the rights of others within the society, they would be dealt with swiftly and with as much of a resemblance of justice as is possible.

As the years pass, the most intelligent among society would create new technologies that even the old world had never seen. Word would reach nation-states and city-states across the continents of an anarchist community that has grown to tens of thousands of people and has created these amazing technologies the world had never seen before. Tens of thousands would turn into hundreds of thousands, and new anarcho-capitalist societies would be created. These societies would have grown exponentially faster and created vastly more wealth than the other nations and city-states. Some statist societies would covet the wealth of these anarcho-capitalist societies while rejecting their ideals. They would attempt to conquer them and might succeed in overtaking some of the smaller ones. Ultimately though, the cultural pride of individual liberty and self-ownership would not tolerate such egregious violations of natural law, and would make the Spirit of 1776 look like merely a hypothetical fantasy created by some of the more radical Mensheviks in order to live vicariously through the Bolsheviks. Armed with their pride and weaponry of the highest quality, the anarcho-capitalists would defeat the tyrants with relative ease.

In the opening chapter, I said, "Liberty will only die if we let her." The sad truth of the matter, however, is that should the preceding anecdote come true, it would mark the birth of Liberty herself as she has never actually existed. As previously stated, every state no matter how small is tyrannical from the moment it is created, but it is also destined to fail. Every state that has ever existed, save for the ones currently in existence, has come to a bloody end. As of this writing, the oldest sovereign nation is San Marino (established in 1600), and the youngest is South Sudan (established in 2011). The earliest documented state was ancient Sumer, formed around 6,500 years ago. This makes San Marino's lifespan around only 6.4% of the total time the state has existed.

Since the creation of the state, literally thousands of sovereign nations, states, empires, and kingdoms have come into existence, only to be overthrown by their people and retried or conquered by another. They say the definition of insanity is continuing to do the same thing and expecting a different outcome. Liberty has never been anything more than just an idea, a seed that has been sowed in the minds of individuals, but never watered. Should the tree of liberty ever be allowed to sprout, the fruits she will eventually bear will be so divine, that nothing in the universe could serve as an acceptable substitute.

Made in the USA
Columbia, SC
18 August 2021

43167889R00117